James and the Giant Peach

Contents

원서 읽는 단어장 소개 ········· 4
이 책의 구성 ········· 6
영어 원서 읽기 전문가가 대답해주는 FAQ ········· 10

Chapter 1-5

Comprehension Quiz ········· 14
Build Your Vocabulary ········· 24
Crossword Puzzle ········· 32

Chapter 6-10

Comprehension Quiz ········· 34
Build Your Vocabulary ········· 44
Crossword Puzzle ········· 48

Chapter 11-15

Comprehension Quiz ········· 50
Build Your Vocabulary ········· 60
Crossword Puzzle ········· 66

Chapter 16-20

    Comprehension Quiz · · · · · · · · · · 68

    Build Your Vocabulary · · · · · · · · · · 78

    Crossword Puzzle · · · · · · · · · · 88

Chapter 21-25

    Comprehension Quiz · · · · · · · · · · 90

    Build Your Vocabulary · · · · · · · · · · 98

    Crossword Puzzle · · · · · · · · · · 104

Chapter 26-30

    Comprehension Quiz · · · · · · · · · · 106

    Build Your Vocabulary · · · · · · · · · · 116

    Crossword Puzzle · · · · · · · · · · 124

Chapter 31-39

    Comprehension Quiz · · · · · · · · · · 126

    Build Your Vocabulary · · · · · · · · · · 138

    Crossword Puzzle · · · · · · · · · · 144

Answers

    Comprehension Quiz Answers · · · · · · · · · · 148

    Crossword Puzzle Answers · · · · · · · · · · 150

원서 읽는 단어장 소개

누구나 추천하는 최고의 영어 공부법, 영어 원서 읽기!

최근 영어 원서 읽기가 영어 공부법으로 주목받고 있습니다. 영어를 많이 접하는 것이 영어 실력을 향상시키는 가장 바람직한 방법이라는 공감대가 형성되면서, 쉽고 저렴하게 영어를 접할 수 있는 '원서 읽기'가 그 대안으로 각광받고 있는 것이지요.

실제로도 영어 좀 한다는 사람들이 원서 읽기를 추천하거나, 어린 아이들이 엄마표 영어 연수 등을 통해 원서를 읽는 많은 사례들을 인터넷 상에서 쉽게 찾아볼 수 있습니다.

원서 읽기를 위한 최고의 친구, 『원서 읽는 단어장』!!

원서 읽기가 영어 공부를 하는 좋은 수단이긴 하지만, 한 번쯤 원서를 읽어 본 독자들은 대부분 다음과 같은 고민을 하곤 합니다.

> 누가 여기 나오는 단어 좀 찾아주면 안 되나?
> 모르는 단어가 나올 때마다 사전을 찾을 수도 없고,
> 그렇다고 그냥 지나치자니 뭔가 찜찜한데...
>
> 지금 내가 제대로 읽고 이해하고 있는 걸까?
> 번역된 책을 찾아서 일일이 대조할 수도 없고,
> 뭔가 확인할 방법이 있었으면 좋겠는데...

이런 문제를 해결해주고자, 여기 『원서 읽는 단어장』이 왔습니다!
원서 읽는 단어장은, 영어 원서에 나온 어려운 어휘들을 완벽히 정리해서

원서 읽기의 부담감을 줄이고 보다 효과적으로 영어 실력을 쌓을 수 있도록 도와주는 책입니다. 또한 이해력을 점검하는 Comprehension Quiz를 통해 내가 원서를 정확히 읽고 있는지 확인해볼 수 있습니다.

『원서 읽는 단어장』시리즈를 통해 영어 원서를 보다 쉽고 재미있게 읽고, 영어 실력도 쑥쑥 향상시켜보세요.

이 책은 Roald Dahl(로알드 달)의 대표작 James and the Giant Peach(제임스와 거대 복숭아) 독자들을 위해 만들어졌습니다. 위 영어 원서는 시중 서점 및 인터넷 서점에서 쉽게 구입할 수 있습니다.

이 책의 구성

Comprehension Quiz

원서를 제대로 읽고 이해하고 있는지 측정해보는 간단한 퀴즈입니다.

원어민 Extensive Reading 전문가가 출제한 쉽고 재미있는 문제들로 구성되어 있습니다. 퀴즈를 풀어보고 틀린 부분이 있다면, 제대로 이해한 것이 맞는지 해당 내용을 다시 한 번 점검해봐야겠죠?

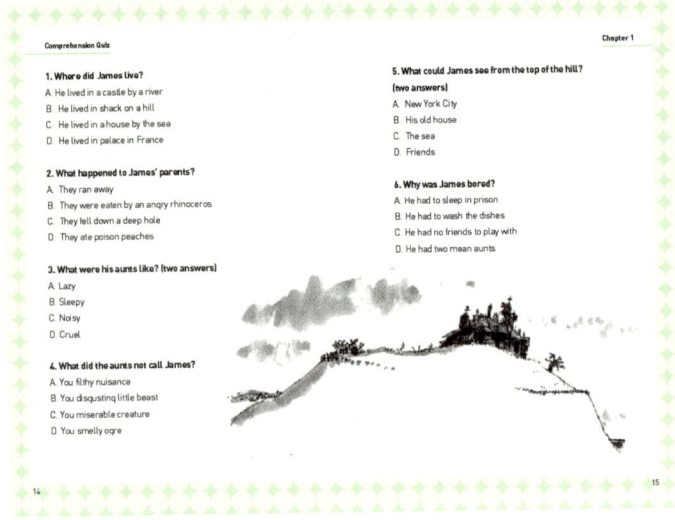

퀴즈는 각 챕터별로 약 5개 안팎의 문제가 출제되어 있습니다.

각 챕터를 읽고 바로 문제를 풀어보는 것도 좋고, 혹은 시간이 되는 대로 쭉 읽은 후 해당 부분만큼 문제를 풀어보는 것도 좋은 방법입니다. 자신의 상황과 스타일에 맞게 적절히 활용하세요!

정답은 148페이지에 있습니다.

Build your Vocabulary

원서에 등장하는 어려운 어휘가 정리되어 있습니다.

단어는 각 챕터별로, 원서에서 단어가 등장하는 순서 그대로 정리되어 있으며, [빈도-스펠링-발음기호-한글 뜻-영어 뜻] 순으로 표기되어 있습니다.

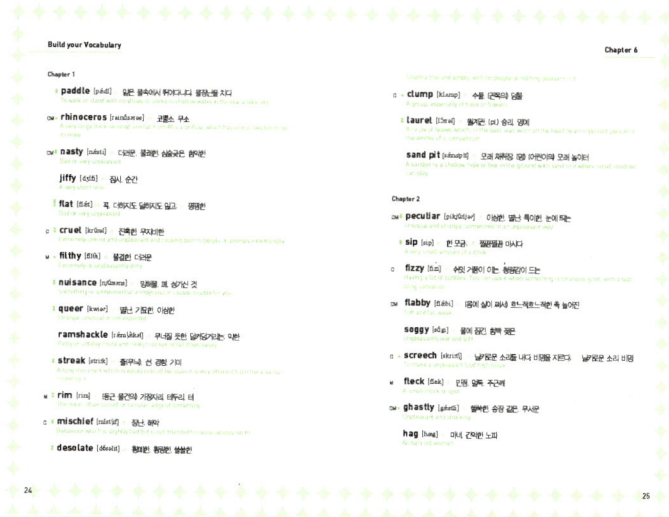

별표(★)가 많을수록 필수 어휘입니다. 또 이전 챕터에서 등장한 중요 어휘가 반복해서 나올 때는 '**복습**'이라고 표시해서 정리했습니다.

특히 로알드 달(Roald Dahl)의 대표 세 작품(Charlie and the Chocolate Factory, Matilda, James and the Giant Peach)의 단어장에는 빈도 표시와 함께 **C**(Charlie and the Chocolate Factory에도 나오는 어휘) 또는 **M**(Matilda에도 나오는 어휘) 표시가 되어 있습니다. 이런 단어를 확실히 암기해두면, 이후 시리즈를 읽을 때 큰 도움이 됩니다.

어휘 목록 중에 아주 기초적인 어휘는 제외되어 있습니다. 원서를 읽을 때 여기 나와 있는 단어 외에도 모르는 어휘가 너무 많다면, '내 영어 수준보다 지나치게 어려운 책을 골랐다'는 의미가 됩니다. 이런 경우에는 일단 더 쉬운 원서에 도전하는 것이 좋은 방법입니다.

　여기 정리된 단어를 일일이 손으로 쓰면서 '암기' 하려고 하지는 마세요! 실질적인 어휘 암기는 원서를 읽으면서 문맥 속에서 단어와 자주 마주칠 때 이루어집니다!

　단어 리스트는 원서를 읽기 전, 후에 눈으로 쭉 살피면서 '단어와 익숙해지도록' 만드는 데 활용하세요. 원서를 읽을 때 단어에서 오는 부담감이 줄어들고, 매우 효율적으로 어휘 실력을 향상시킬 수 있습니다.

Crossword Puzzle

잠시 쉬어가면서 낱말 맞추기 퍼즐을 하는 페이지입니다.
각 문제에 해당하는 단어 스펠링을 가로-세로 빈칸에 맞춰서 채워나가면 됩니다.

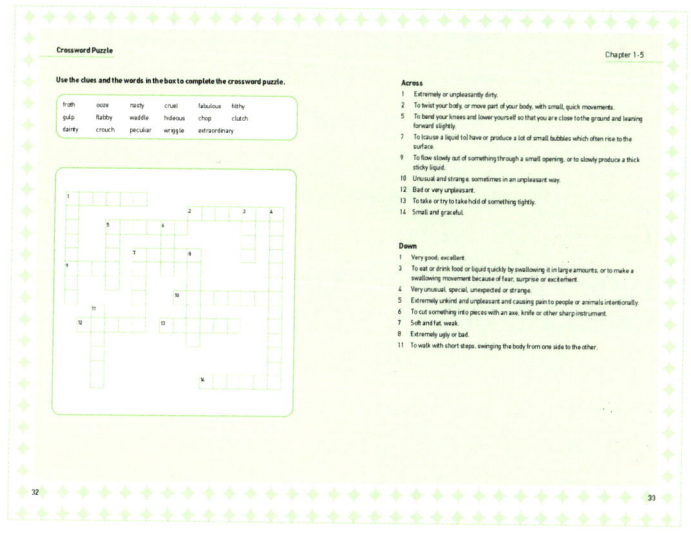

퍼즐의 문제들은 원서에서 반복해서 등장하는 중요 어휘로 구성되어 있습니다. 편안한 마음으로 퍼즐을 풀어보세요! 그러다보면 어휘 실력도 더욱 탄탄하게 다져질 것입니다.

정답은 150페이지에 있습니다.

영어 원서 읽기 전문가가 대답해주는 FAQ

Q. 단어장에 나오는 단어 중에 모르는 단어가 너무 많네요. 전부 외워야 할까요?

A. 모든 단어를 완벽하게 외울 필요는 전혀 없습니다! 원서에 나오는 단어 중에는 보통 상황에는 거의 사용되지 않는 단어도 많고, 심지어 작가가 만든 단어까지 있습니다. 이런 단어들을 철저하게 외우는 것은 정말 비효율적인 일이지요.

일단 원서를 읽기 전에 단어장을 쭉 훑어봅니다. 빈도가 높고 (★ 개수가 많고), 책 안에서 자주 반복되는 단어들 ('복습'이라고 표시되어 있는 단어들)을 우선하여 주의 깊게 살펴보세요. 이 때 모든 단어를 완벽하게 암기할 필요는 없습니다. 가볍게 눈으로 보고 바로 원서 읽기에 들어가세요. 원서를 읽으면서 방금 훑어봤던 단어를 자연히 마주치게 되고, 이런 과정에서 그 단어의 뜻은 물론 쓰이는 상황과 느낌까지 한꺼번에 학습하게 됩니다. 또 원서 읽기를 마치면 그날 읽은 부분에 나오는 단어를 한 번 더 훑어보는 것으로 마무리하세요. 이렇게 단어를 자주 마주치다보면 어휘력을 더 탄탄하게 다질 수 있습니다.

우리는 일반적으로 단어 암기를 할 때, 눈으로 보고, 손으로 쓰고, 입으로 발음하면서, 즉 5감을 활용해서 암기하려고 합니다. 이런 방식의 암기는 매우 좋은 방법이지만, 기초 필수 어휘 외의 다른 단어 암기에도 같은 방식을 적용시키는 것은 너무 비효율적입니다. 자주 쓰이고 중요한 어휘라면 원서를 읽으면서(영어를 폭넓게 접하면서) 많이 만날 수밖에 없고, 굳이 의도하지 않아도 자연스럽게 암기하게 됩니다. 이렇게 '영어를 많이 접하면서' 어휘력을 향상시키는 것이 가장 좋은 단어 학습법입니다.

Q. 저는 말하기도 잘하고 싶은데, 원서 읽기가 도움이 될까요?

A. 물론 원서 읽기는 말하기에도 많은 도움이 됩니다!

유창한 말하기는 모든 영어 학습자의 로망이라고 할 수 있습니다. 하지만 영어 말하기를 원하는 학습자가 쉽게 간과하는 것이 있는데, 그것은 'Input이 없으면 그만한 Output도 없다'는 사실입니다.

영어 말하기는 이미 영어를 많이 접하고 머릿속에 충분한 양이 축적되었을 때야만 자연스럽게 터져 나옵니다. 따라서 영어 말하기의 전제 조건은 일단 '영어를 폭넓게 접할 것, 영어 Input의 양을 충분히 늘릴 것'입니다. 그리고 이렇게 '영어 Input'을 폭발적으로 늘리는 가장 좋은 방법이 바로 영어 원서 읽기입니다! 언제 어디서나 원서를 펴기만 하면 곧바로 영어를 접할 수 있는 환경이 만들어지기 때문이지요.

유창한 말하기를 원하십니까? 그럼 원서를 많이 읽으세요! 아직 말하기가 만족스럽지 않다면 더 열심히 읽으셔야 합니다. 원서를 읽으면서 발견하는 좋은 표현들이나 등장인물들의 대화를 큰 소리로 따라 읽는 것도 매우 좋은 방법입니다. 또 오디오북을 들으면서 성우의 목소리를 최대한 따라하면서 소리 내어 읽는 것도 추천해드립니다. 이런 노력들이 쌓이고 쌓여서 탁월한 말하기 실력으로 돌아올 것입니다.

Q. James and the Giant Peach를 정말 재미있게 읽었어요! 비슷한 수준의 다른 원서 좀 추천해주세요.

A. 일단 기본적으로 같은 저자 Roald Dahl의 다른 책들을 읽어볼 것을 추천해드립니다. 같은 저자가 썼기 때문에 똑같이 재미를 느낄 수 있고, 같은 어휘와 문체가 반복해서 등장하기 때문에 자연스럽게 복습하는 효과를 얻게 됩니다. (Roald Dahl의 다른 책들 역시 「원서 읽는 단어장」으로 꾸준히 출간될 예정입니다.)

이 외에 앤드류 클레멘츠(Andrew Clements)의 책을 추천해드립니다. 그의 작품으로는 「Frindle」, 「The Landry New」 등 다양한 책이 있습니다. 원어민 초등학생을 위해 쓰인 책이긴 하지만, 남녀노소 모두 좋아할 만한 내용에 영어 수준도 무난해서 Roald Dahl의 애독자라면 꼭 한번 읽어볼 만합니다. 또한 미국의 인기 작가 루이스 로리(Lois Lowry)의 「Number the Stars」, 뉴베리상 수상작인 「Sarah, Plain and Tall」도 같은 수준의 추천할 만한 책들입니다.

Comprehension Quiz
Build Your Vocabulary
Crossword Puzzle

Comprehension Quiz

1. Where did James live?

A. He lived in a castle by a river

B. He lived in shack on a hill

C. He lived in a house by the sea

D. He lived in palace in France

2. What happened to James' parents?

A. They ran away

B. They were eaten by an angry rhinoceros

C. They fell down a deep hole

D. They ate poison peaches

3. What were his aunts like? (two answers)

A. Lazy

B. Sleepy

C. Noisy

D. Cruel

4. What did the aunts not call James?

A. You filthy nuisance

B. You disgusting little beast

C. You miserable creature

D. You smelly ogre

Chapter 1

5. What could James see from the top of the hill? (two answers)

A. New York City

B. His old house

C. The sea

D. Friends

6. Why was James bored?

A. He had to sleep in prison

B. He had to wash the dishes

C. He had no friends to play with

D. He had two mean aunts

Comprehension Quiz

1. How many peculiar things were about to happen?

A. 1

B. 3

C. 5

D. 6

2. What does Aunt Sponge look like?

A. Short and fat with piggy eyes

B. Tall and bony with steel rimmed glasses

C. Young and kind with soft skin

D. Thick and strong with a bull neck

3. What do Spiker and Sponge not say about each other?

A. You would make a lovely Frankenstein

B. Don't forget how much your tummy shows

C. You're only bones and skin

D. That's it. You are prettier than me. You win!

Chapter 2

4. What does James dream about? (two answers)

A. Playing in the wet sand and splashing around

B. Chopping wood and sweating

C. Drinking lemonade and looking in a mirror

D. Walking in the cool woods and picking flowers

Comprehension Quiz

1. Who did James meet?

A. Aunt Spiker come to beat him

B. A small bald man with a black beard and a creaky voice

C. A giant bug

D. His mother and father

2. How close did the man stand to James? (two answers)

A. So close James could smell the man's breath

B. So close he could feel the man's nose touching his forehead

C. So close that the man was behind James

D. So close that James could see in the man's nose

3. What did the man give to James?

A. A bag of candy

B. A picture of the sea

C. A bag of magic crocodile tongues

D. A bag of magic peaches

4. How much magic is in tiny green things?

A. More than in a magician's wand

B. More than in a mother's heart

C. More than in a child's smile

D. More than in the whole world

Chapter 3

5. What were tiny green things made of? (two answers)

A. The beak of an eagle

B. Gizzard of a pig

C. Porcupine juice

D. A pinch of salt

Comprehension Quiz

1. What should James not do to use the magic?

A. Put the magic crocodile tongues in water

B. Add 10 hairs from his own head

C. Drink the whole jug in one gulp

D. Boil himself in steaming water

2. What magic things will happen to James? (two answers)

A. Marvelous things

B. Fantabulous things

C. Unbelievable things

D. Glorious things

3. What will happen if James drops the little green things?

A. They will bounce back into the bag

B. They will work their magic on something else

C. They will disappear

D. They will pop like little bombs

Chapter 4

4. On what will the magic not work?

A. Trees

B. Bugs

C. Rocks

D. Animals

Comprehension Quiz

1. Where did James plan to make the magic drink?

A. In the well

B. Under the peach tree

C. In the kitchen

D. In his room

Chapter 5

2. Where did James drop the bag of precious magic?

A. On Aunt Spiker's head

B. In Aunt Sponge's dress

C. On the peach tree

D. Under the peach tree

3. What did the magic things do?

A. They burrowed into the earth

B. They bounced back into the bag

C. They ran around in circles

D. They flew away

4. What did Aunt Sponge threaten to do to James?

A. Beat him with a broom

B. Make him sleep under the tree all night

C. Give him a massage

D. Put him down the well for the night

Build your Vocabulary

Chapter 1

paddle [pǽdl] *v.* 얕은 물속에서 뛰어다니다; 물장난을 치다
To walk or stand with no shoes or socks in shallow water in the sea, a lake, etc.

rhinoceros [rainɑ́sərəs] *n.* 코뿔소, 무소
A very large thick-skinned animal from Africa or Asia, which has one or two horns on its nose.

nasty [nǽsti] *a.* 더러운, 불쾌한; 심술궂은, 험악한
Bad or very unpleasant.

jiffy [dʒífi] *n.* 잠시, 순간
A very short time.

flat [flǽt] *ad.* 꼭, 더하지도 덜하지도 않고; *a.* 평평한
Having a level surface, not curved or sloping.

cruel [krúːəl] *a.* 잔혹한, 무자비한
Extremely unkind and unpleasant and causing pain to people or animals intentionally.

filthy [fílθi] *a.* 불결한, 더러운
Extremely or unpleasantly dirty.

nuisance [njúːsəns] *n.* 방해물, 폐, 성가신 것
Something or someone that annoys you or causes trouble for you.

queer [kwiər] *a.* 별난, 기묘한, 이상한
Strange, unusual or not expected.

ramshackle [rǽmʃæ̀kəl] *a.* 무너질 듯한, 덜커덩거리는; 약한
Badly or untidily made and likely to break or fall down easily.

streak [striːk] *n.* 줄(무늬), 선; 경향, 기미
A long thin mark or line that is a different colour from the surface it is on.

rim [rim] *n.* (둥근 물건의) 가장자리, 테두리, 테
The outer, often curved or circular, edge of something.

mischief [místʃif] *n.* 장난; 해악
Behaviour which is slightly bad but is not intended to cause serious harm.

desolate [désəlit] *a.* 황폐한, 황량한, 쓸쓸한
Unattractive and empty, with no people or nothing pleasant in it.

Chapter 1-5

C ★ **clump** [klʌmp] *n.* 수풀, (관목의) 덤불
A group, especially of trees or flowers.

⁚ **laurel** [lɔ́:rəl] *n.* [식물] 월계수
A small evergreen tree which has shiny leaves and small black fruit.

sand pit [sǽndpìt] *n.* 모래 채취장; (영) (어린이의) 모래 놀이터
A sandpit is a shallow hole or box in the ground with sand in it where small children can play.

⁚ **gaze** [geiz] *v.* 뚫어지게 보다, 응시하다; *n.* 주시, 응시
To look steadily at someone or something for a long time.

★ **wistful** [wístfəl] *a.* 탐내는; 동경하는 (wistfully *ad.* 동경하며, 생각에 잠겨)
Sad and thinking about something that is impossible or in the past.

Chapter 2

CM **peculiar** [pikjú:ljər] *a.* 이상한, 별난; 특이한, 눈에 띄는
Unusual and strange, sometimes in an unpleasant way.

M ⁚ **chop** [tʃɔp] *vt.* (도끼·식칼 등으로) 자르다, 패다; 잘게 썰다
To cut something into pieces with an axe, knife or other sharp instrument.

⁚ **sip** [sip] *n.* 한 모금; *vt.* 찔끔찔끔 마시다
A very small amount of a drink.

C **fizzy** [fízi] *a.* 쉬잇 거품이 이는, 청량감이 드는
Having a lot of bubbles; You can use it when something is strangely good, with a bubbling sensation.

CM **flabby** [flǽbi] *a.* (몸에 살이 쪄서) 흐느적흐느적한, 축 늘어진
Soft and fat, weak.

soggy [sɔ́gi] *a.* 물에 잠긴, 흠뻑 젖은
Unpleasantly wet and soft.

C ★ **screech** [skri:tʃ] *vt.* 날카로운 소리를 내다, 비명을 지르다; *n.* 날카로운 소리, 비명
To make a unpleasant loud high noise.

M **fleck** [flek] *n.* 반점, 얼룩, 주근깨
A small mark or spot.

Build your Vocabulary

CM ★ **ghastly** [gǽstli] *a.* 핼쑥한, 송장 같은, 무서운
Unpleasant and shocking.

hag [hæg] *n.* 마녀, 간악한 노파
An ugly old woman.

★ **hideous** [hídiəs] *a.* 끔찍한, 무시무시한, 소름끼치는, 섬뜩한
Extremely ugly or bad.

C ‡ **feast** [fiːst] *n.* 축제, 진수성찬 *v.* 축연을 베풀다, 진수성찬을 먹다
A day on which a religious event or person is remembered and celebrated.

‡ **behold** [bihóuld] *vt.* 보다
If you behold someone or something, you see them.

‡ **heavenly** [hévənli] *a.* 하늘의; 천국의[같은]; 거룩한
Of heaven.

M ‡ **dainty** [déinti] *a.* 섬약[섬세]한, 가냘픈; 까다로운; 맛좋은
Small and graceful.

C **tummy** [tʌ́mi] *n.* (유아어) 배 (stomach)
The stomach, or the lower front part of the body.

curvy [kə́ːrvi] *a.* (길 등이) 구불구불한, 굽은 (데가 많은)
Containing a lot of curves.

beauteous [bjúːtiəs] (=beautiful) *a.* 믿을 수 없을[황홀할] 정도로 아름다운
Very attractive to look at; beautiful.

‡ **radiant** [réidiənt] *a.* 빛나는, 밝은
Showing great happiness, love or health.

pimple [pímpl] *n.* 여드름, 뾰루지
A small raised spot on the skin which is temporary.

★ **trout** [traut] *n.* 송어
A fish that is a popular food, especially a brown type that lives in rivers and lakes or a silver type that lives in the sea but returns to rivers to reproduce.

‡ **resign** [rizáin] *v.* 사직하다, 그만두다; 단념하다
To give up a job or position by telling your employer that you are leaving.

Chapter 1-5

aching [éikiŋ] *a.* 쑤시는, 아리는; 마음 아픈
If you ache or a part of your body aches, you feel a steady, fairly strong pain.

blunt [blʌnt] *a.* 무딘, 날 없는; 무뚝뚝한, 퉁명스러운
A blunt object has a rounded or flat end rather than a sharp one.

tricycle [tráisikəl] *n.* (어린이용의) 세 바퀴 자전거; 삼륜 오토바이
A cycle with two wheels at the back and one at the front.

c **ooze** [u:z] *a.* 스며 나오다, 새어나오다 (oozy *a.* 스며 나오는, 새는)
To flow slowly out of something through a small opening, or to slowly produce a thick sticky liquid.

overwhelm [òuvərhwélm] *vt.* 압도하다, 제압하다; 질리게 하다
To defeat someone or something by using a lot of force.

steel [sti:l] *n.* 강철; *vt.* 강철을 입히다, 단단히 하다
A very strong metal which is made mainly from iron.

spectacle [spektəkəl] *n.* 광경, 장관; (pl.) 안경
An unusual or unexpected event or situation which attracts attention, interest or disapproval.

c **brute** [brú:t] *n.* 짐승, 야만인; *a.* 잔인한, 야만적인, 무정한
A rough and sometimes violent man.

Chapter 3

rustle [rʌ́səl] *vi.* 살랑살랑 소리 내다, 바스락거리다; 활발히 움직이다
If things such as paper or leaves rustle, or if you rustle them, they move about and make a soft, dry sound.

bristly [brísəli] *a.* 털이 억센; 빽빽이[꼿꼿이] 들어선; 화낸
Bristly hair is thick and rough.

whisker [hwískər] *n.* 구레나룻, 수염
Any of the long, stiff hairs growing on the face of a cat, mouse or other mammal.

creaky [krí:ki] *a.* 삐걱삐걱하는, 삐걱거리는
Describes something that creaks.

c **beckon** [békən] *v.* 손짓[고갯짓·몸짓]으로 부르다, 신호하다
To move your hand or head in a way that tells someone to come nearer.

Build your Vocabulary

- **hobble** [hάbəl] *vi.* 절뚝거리며 걷다
  To walk in an awkward way, usually because the feet or legs are injured.

  to and fro [túːɑnfróu] *a.* 이리저리[앞뒤로] 움직이는, 동요하는
  In one direction and then in the opposite direction, a repeated number of times.

  musty [mʌ́sti] *a.* 곰팡이 핀; 케케묵은, 진부한
  Smelling unpleasantly old and slightly wet.

- **stale** [stéil] *a.* (음식 따위가) 상한, 신선하지 않은
  Not fresh and new; boring because too familiar.

  mildew [míldjuː] *n.* 곰팡이
  A black, green or whitish area caused by a fungus that grows on things such as plants, paper, cloth or buildings, usually if the conditions are warm and wet.

- **cellar** [sélər] *n.* 지하실, 땅광, 움
  A room under the ground floor of a building, usually used for storage.

- **tilt** [tilt] *vi.* 기울이다, 뒤집다
  To (cause to) move into a sloping position.

CM **extraordinary** [ikstrɔ́ːrdənèri] *a.* 대단한, 비상한, 비범한; 터무니없는
  Very unusual, special, unexpected or strange.

C **luminous** [lúːmənəs] *a.* 빛을 내는, 빛나는
  Producing or reflecting bright light.

  glow [glóu] *n.* 달아오름, 온기, 행복감
  Intensity of feeling, especially pleasant feeling.

  whisper [hwíspər] *v.* 속이다, 소곤거리다; *n.* 속삭임
  To speak very quietly to somebody so that other people cannot hear what you are saying.

  stir [stə́ːr] *v.* 휘젓다, 움직이다, 흔들다; 흥분시키다
  To mix a liquid or other substance by moving an object such as a spoon in a circular pattern.

- **murmur** [mə́ːrmər] *v.* 중얼거리다
  To speak or say very quietly.

CM **crouch** [kráutʃ] *v.* 몸을 구부리다, 쭈그리다, 웅크리다
  To bend your knees and lower yourself so that you are close to the ground and leaning forward slightly.

Chapter 1-5

slimy [sláimi] *a.* 진흙투성이의; 끈적끈적한; 불쾌한, 더러운
Slimy substances are thick, wet, and unpleasant.

gizzard [gízərd] *n.* (구어·익살) (사람의) 내장 (특히 위장)

‡ **beak** [bíːk] *n.* 새의 부리
The hard pointed part of a bird's mouth.

★ **porcupine** [pɔ́ːrkjəpàin] *n.* [동물] 호저 (부드러운 털과 뻣뻣한 가시털이 빽빽이 나 있으며 위험이 닥치면 몸을 밤송이처럼 동그랗게 한다.)
An animal with a protective covering of long sharp quills.

Chapter 4

CM ‡ **clutch** [klʌtʃ] *v.* 꽉 잡다, 붙들다
To take or try to take hold of something tightly.

CM ‡ **froth** [frɔ́θ] *n.* 거품 *v.* 거품을 일으키다
To have or produce a lot of small bubbles which often rise to the surface.

jugful [dʒʌ́gful] *n.* 주전자(잔) 하나(의 분량)

M ★ **gulp** [gʌlp] *v.* 꿀꺽꿀꺽 마시다, 쭉 삼켜버리다
To eat or drink food or liquid quickly by swallowing it in large amounts, or to make a swallowing movement because of fear, surprise or excitement.

churn [tʃəːrn] *v.* 휘젓다; 괴롭히다, 고민하게 하다
If your stomach is churning, you feel ill, usually because you are nervous.

‡ **marvelous** [máːrvələs] *a.* 놀라운, 믿기 어려운; (구어) 훌륭한, 우수한
Extremely good.

CM **fabulous** [fǽbjələs] *a.* 굉장한, 멋진; 황당무계한, 믿어지지 않는
Very good; excellent.

‡ **miserable** [mízərəbəl] *a.* 불쌍한, 비참한, 불행한
Unpleasant and causing unhappiness.

Chapter 5

stinging [stíŋiŋ] *a.* 찌르는, 쏘는; 쏘는 듯한, 날카로운
To cause sharp but usually temporary pain.

Build your Vocabulary

* **nettle** [nétl] *n.* [식물] 쐐기풀
  A wild plant with heart-shaped leaves that are covered in hairs which sting.

C * **swerve** [swəːrv] *v.* 벗어나다, 빗나가다; *n.* 벗어남, 빗나감
  To change direction, especially suddenly.

  burst open *idiom* 왈칵[홱] 열다; 활짝 피다[벌어지다]
  When a door or lid bursts open, it opens very suddenly and violently because someone pushes it or there is great pressure behind it.

C * **scatter** [skǽtər] *v.* 흩뿌리다, 뿔뿔이 흩어지다
  To depart or send off in different directions.

C * **wriggle** [rígəl] *v.* 꿈틀거리다, 몸부림치다; *n.* 몸부림침, 꿈틀거림
  To twist your body, or move part of your body, with small, quick movements.

* **burrow** [bə́ːrou] *n.* 굴, 은신처; *v.* 굴을 파다, 굴에 살다[숨다]
  A hole in the ground dug by an animal such as a rabbit, especially to live in.

  scrabble [skrǽbəl] *v.* (손톱으로) 할퀴다; 휘젓다
  To use your fingers to quickly find something that you cannot see.

* **frantically** [frǽntikəli] *ad.* 미친 듯이, 광포하게, 광란하여
  Behaving in a wild and uncontrolled way.

* **vanish** [vǽniʃ] *v.* 사라지다, 자취를 감추다
  If someone or something vanishes, they disappear suddenly.

  centipede [séntəpìːd] *n.* [동물] 지네
  A small, long, thin animal with many legs.

* **grim** [grim] *a.* 엄한, 엄격한; 험상스러운, 무서운
  Very unpleasant or ugly.

  pulpy [pʌ́lpi] *a.* 걸쭉한, 흐늘흐늘한
  Something that is pulpy is soft, smooth, and wet, often because it has been crushed or beaten.

* **jellyfish** [dʒélifiʃ] *n.* 해파리
  A sea animal with a soft oval almost transparent body.

M **waddle** [wádl] *vi.* 뒤뚱거리며 걷다, 어기적어기적 걷다
  To walk with short steps, swinging the body from one side to the other.

wheeze [hwiːz] *n.* (영·구어) 계략, 계획; *v.* 씨근거리다, 헐떡이며 말하다
A clever trick or plan.

hideous [hídiəs] *a.* 끔찍한, 무시무시한, 소름끼치는, 섬뜩한
Extremely ugly or bad.

brat [bræt] *n.* (경멸적) 선머슴, 개구쟁이
A child, especially one who behaves badly.

woodpile [wúdpàil] *n.* 장작[땔나무]을 쌓은 더미
A woodpile is a pile of wood that is intended to be burnt on a fire as fuel.

Crossword Puzzle

Use the clues and the words in the box to complete the crossword puzzle.

froth	ooze	nasty	cruel	fabulous	filthy
gulp	flabby	waddle	hideous	chop	clutch
dainty	crouch	peculiar	wriggle	extraordinary	

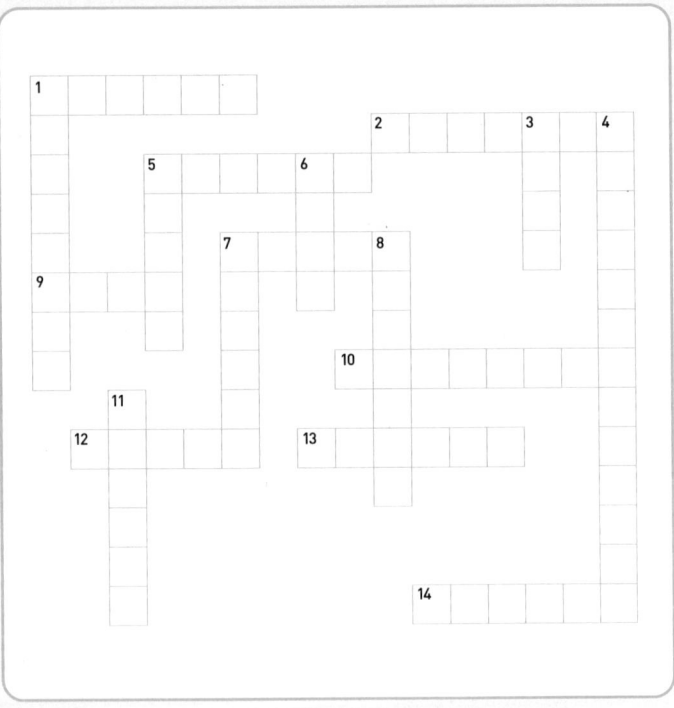

Across

1. Extremely or unpleasantly dirty.
2. To twist your body, or move part of your body, with small, quick movements.
5. To bend your knees and lower yourself so that you are close to the ground and leaning forward slightly.
7. To have or produce a lot of small bubbles which often rise to the surface.
9. To flow slowly out of something through a small opening, or to slowly produce a thick sticky liquid.
10. Unusual and strange, sometimes in an unpleasant way.
12. Bad or very unpleasant.
13. To take or try to take hold of something tightly.
14. Small and graceful.

Down

1. Very good; excellent.
3. To eat or drink food or liquid quickly by swallowing it in large amounts, or to make a swallowing movement because of fear, surprise or excitement.
4. Very unusual, special, unexpected or strange.
5. Extremely unkind and unpleasant and causing pain to people or animals intentionally.
6. To cut something into pieces with an axe, knife or other sharp instrument.
7. Soft and fat, weak.
8. Extremely ugly or bad.
11. To walk with short steps, swinging the body from one side to the other.

Comprehension Quiz

1. What did Spiker see in the tree?

A. A blossom

B. A pear

C. A caterpillar

D. A peach

2. Where was the peach growing?

A. On the ground where James dropped the magic creatures

B. On the tree trunk

C. On the highest branch

D. In the air

3. What did James think was going to happen?

A. He was going to see something peculiar

B. He was going to be beaten

C. He was going to chop some more wood

D. He was going to cry because he lost his bag of magic

4. What does Aunt Sponge tell James to do?

A. Cut down the tree

B. Take a picture of the peach

C. Climb up and get the peach for his aunts

D. Eat the peach

5. What do the Aunts want to do with the peach?

A. Let it grow

B. Give it to James

C. Plant it, so they can have two peach trees

D. Split it in half and eat it

6. What is special about the peach?

A. It looks ripe

B. It is growing so fast you can see it

C. It looks like Aunt Sponge

D. It is singing

Comprehension Quiz

1. Which one is not a size of the peach?

A. As big as a melon

B. As big as a pumpkin

C. As big as Aunt Sponge

D. As big as a castle

2. What did the Aunts say about the still growing peach? (two answers)

A. Halleluyah!

B. Magnifico Splendifico

C. It's the most beautiful thing I have ever seen

D. I have seen bigger peaches before

3. Why didn't the peach fall off of the tree? (two answers)

A. Because the branch bent

B. Because the peach was not heavy

C. Because Aunts are standing under it

D. Because the peach is as tall as the tree

Chapter 7

4. Why did Aunt Spiker say to not eat the peach?

A. It will get bigger

B. They can make a lot of money

C. It is not ripe

D. She is not hungry

Comprehension Quiz

1. What did the Aunts do after the news about the peach?

A. They had James put up a fence

B. They gave people rides in helicopters

C. They cut up the peach and sold it

D. They charged people to see the peach

2. How much did the Aunts charge? (two answers)

A. One shilling for adults

B. One half shilling for babies

C. Ten shillings for cameras

D. One hundred shillings for James

Chapter 8

3. Why couldn't James play with the other children who came to see the peach?

A. He would steal the money

B. He would sell a lot of tickets

C. He would stay at home

D. He would mess everything up

4. Why didn't the Aunts make dinner for James?

A. They were tired from working all day

B. They were out of food

C. They were too busy counting their money

D. They were busy watching TV

5. What did the Aunts make James do at night?

A. Water the peach

B. Pick up all of the trash

C. Check the fence for holes

D. Guard the peach from thieves

Comprehension Quiz

1. How did James feel when he first went outside?

A. Hungry because he had no dinner

B. Happy to be away from his Aunts

C. Afraid of the dark

D. Sad because he had to pick up trash

2. What did James think after he got shivers on his back?

A. I am cold

B. Something dangerous is going to happen

C. Something stranger than before is going to happen

D. The aunts are going to unlock the door and feed me.

3. James saw the peach and felt something pulling him. What was it similar to?

A. Like a rope

B. Like a truck

C. Like a magnet

D. Like a bulldozer

4. What did James see when he rubbed his cheek on the peach?

A. A hole in ground

B. A hole in the peach

C. A hole in the tree

D. A hole in his shoe

Comprehension Quiz

1. What did James do in the tunnel? (two answers)

A. Meet a fox

B. Drink the peach juice

C. Eat some of the tunnel wall

D. Put some peach in his pocket for later

Chapter 10

2. What did James bang his head on?

A. A rock

B. A wall

C. The tunnel

D. The stone

3. What did James hear when he entered the room?

A. Go pick up the trash

B. This is my peach

C. Hello, we have been waiting for you

D. Hello, we are going to eat you

4. How did James feel when he saw who was in the room?

A. So scared he went completely white

B. Surprised to meet someone new

C. Happy to make new friends

D. So sad he cried his eyes out

Build your Vocabulary

Chapter 6

- **tease** [tíːz] *v.* 놀리다, 희롱하다
  To laugh at or make fun of someone annoyingly.

- **gracious** [gréiʃəs] *a.* 상냥한, 정중한
  Behaving in a pleasant, polite, calm way.

- **peculiar** [pikjúːljər] *a.* 이상한, 별난; 특이한, 눈에 띄는
  Unusual and strange, sometimes in an unpleasant way.

- **faint** [feint] *a.* 희미한, 어렴풋한; 기절할 것 같은; *vi.* 기절하다
  If you faint, you lose consciousness for a short time.

- **still** [stil] *a.* 조용한, 정지한; *ad.* 아직(도), 여전히
  (stillness *n.* 고요, 정적)
  Staying in the same position; not moving.

- **tiptoe** [típtòu] *n.* 발끝; *vi.* 발끝으로 걷다; 발돋움하다
  On your toes with the heel of your foot lifted off the ground.

- **ripe** [ráip] *a.* 익은, 여문
  Completely developed and ready to be collected or eaten.

- **lick** [lik] *vt.* 핥다; 스치다, 넘실거리다
  To move the tongue across the surface of something.

- **bulge** [bʌldʒ] *v.* 부풀다, 불룩해지다, 부풀리다
  To stick out in a round shape.

- **swell** [swel] *v.* 부풀다, 붓다, 팽창하다 (up, out); 증가하다
  To become larger and rounder than usual; to (cause to) increase in size or amount.

Chapter 7

- **terrifico** '엄청나군!' (terrific) 로알드 달이 만들어낸 감탄사

- **magnifico** '굉장한데!' (magnificent) 로알드 달이 만들어낸 감탄사

- **splendifico** '근사한걸!' (splendid) 로알드 달이 만들어낸 감탄사

- **spellbound** [spélbàund] *a.* 마법에 걸린, 넋을 잃은
  Extremely interested in something.

Chapter 6-10

M **twerp** [twəːrp] *n.* (구어) 너절한 놈
A stupid person.

: **inspect** [inspékt] *vt.* 검사하다, 조사하다
To examine something carefully in order to find out more about it.

midget [mídʒit] *n.* 난쟁이, 꼬마; *a.* 극소형의
A very small person.

M : **patch** [pætʃ] *n.* 헝겊 조각; 단편; *vt.* 헝겊을 대고 깁다; 주워 맞추다
A small area which is different in some way from the area that surrounds it.

CM **hunk** [hʌŋk] *n.* 두꺼운 조각, 큰 덩어리
A large thick piece, especially of food.

. **trickle** [tríkəl] *n.* 물방울 *vi.* 똑똑 떨어지다, 졸졸 흐르다
If liquid trickles somewhere, it flows slowly and without force in a thin line.

C : **sly** [slái] *a.* 은밀한, 음흉한; 익살맞은 (slyly *ad.* 음흉하게, 장난스럽게)
A sly look or expression shows that you know something that other people do not know.

Chapter 8

wildfire [wáildfàiər] *n.* (옛날 적의 배에 불지르기 위해 사용한) 연소물, 도깨비불
A fire which is burning strongly and out of control on an area of grass or bushes in the countryside.

: **marvel** [máːrvəl] *n.* 놀라운 일[사람], 불가사의함; *vi.* 놀라다, 경탄하다
To show or experience great surprise or admiration.

: **carpenter** [káːrpəntər] *n.* 목수, 목공
A person whose job is making and repairing wooden objects and structures.

M . **crafty** [kræfti] *a.* 교활한, 간악한, 교묘한
Clever, especially in a dishonest or secretive way.

seething [síːðiŋ] *a.* 펄펄 끓는; 소용돌이치는; 들끓는
To be full of a lot of people or animals, especially when they are all moving around.

C : **glimpse** [glimps] *n.* 흘끗 보임, 일견
If you get a glimpse of something, you see them very briefly and not very well.

CM . **wasp** [wɑsp] *n.* 장수말벌; 성질 잘 내는 사람

Build your Vocabulary

C **swarm** [swɔːrm] *vi.* 떼를 짓다; *n.* 떼, 무리
When people swarm somewhere, they move there in a large group.

greedy [gríːdi] *a.* 탐욕스러운, 욕심 사나운, 몹시 탐내는
Wanting a lot more food, money, etc. than you need.

peep [piːp] *vi.* 엿보다, 슬쩍 들여다보다; *n.* 엿봄, 훔쳐보기
To secretly look at something for a short time, usually through a hole.

wander [wɑ́ndər] *v.* 거닐다, 돌아다니다
To walk around slowly in a relaxed way or without any clear direction.

cut it out *idiom* (구어) (명령형으로) 귀찮다!; 그만둬!, 닥쳐!

M **snap** [snæp] *v.* 날카롭게[느닷없이] 말하다; 홱 잡다, 탁 소리 내다, 덥석 물다
To say something suddenly in an angry way.

millionaire [mìljənɛ́ər] *n.* 백만장자, 큰 부자
A person whose wealth is at least 1,000,000 in their country's money.

slam [slæm] *v.* (문 등을) 탕[쾅] 닫다[닫히다]; 털썩 내려놓다
To move against a hard surface with force and usually a loud noise.

Chapter 9

trembling [trémbliŋ] *a.* 떠는, 전율하는
To shake slightly, usually because you are cold, frightened, or very emotional.

twig [twig] *n.* 잔가지, 가는 가지
A small thin branch of a tree or bush, especially one removed from the tree or bush and without any leaves.

C **dazzle** [dǽzəl] *vt.* 눈부시게 하다; 현혹시키다, 감탄시키다
If light dazzles you, it makes you unable to see for a short time.

C **glint** [glint] *v.* 반짝이다, 빛나다; *n.* 반짝임, 섬광
To produce small bright flashes of light reflected from a surface.

CM **tremendous** [triméndəs] *a.* 거대한, 대단한; 엄청난, 무서운
Very great in amount or level, or extremely good.

C **shiver** [ʃívər] *v.* (추위·공포로) 후들후들 떨다
To shake slightly because you are cold or frightened.

Chapter 6-10

dew [dju:] *n.* 이슬; *v.* 이슬로 적시다
Drops of water that form on the ground and other surfaces outside during the night.

C **twinkle** [twíŋkəl] *v.* 반짝반짝 빛나다
To shine repeatedly strongly then weakly, as if flashing on and off very quickly.

magnet [mǽgnit] *n.* 자석, 자철
A piece of iron or other material which attracts iron towards it.

furry [fə́:ri] *a.* 부드러운 털의; 모피로 덮인[만든]
Covered with fur.

Chapter 10

M **crawl** [krɔ:l] *vi.* 기어가다, 느릿느릿 가다
To move slowly, especially with the body stretched out along the ground.

C **damp** [dæmp] *a.* 축축한
Slightly wet, especially in a way that is not pleasant or comfortable.

murky [mə́:rki] *a.* 어두운, (안개·연기가) 자욱한
Dark and difficult to see through.

bittersweet [bítərswìːt] *a.* 달콤 씁쓸한; 괴로움도 있고 즐거움도 있는
Tasting both bitter and sweet.

soggy [sɑ́gi] *a.* 물에 잠긴, 함빡 젖은
Unpleasantly wet and soft.

jagged [dʒǽgid] *a.* 깔쭉깔쭉한, 톱니 같은, 지그재그의
Rough and uneven, with sharp points.

C **groove** [gru:v] *n.* 홈, 바퀴 자국; 관례, 습관
A long narrow hollow space cut into a surface.

bolt [bóult] *vi.* 뛰어 나가다, 도망치다
To move suddenly and quickly.

Crossword Puzzle

Use the clues and the words in the box to complete the crossword puzzle.

lick	soggy	swell	swarm	crawl	snap	spellbound
hunk	shiver	crafty	dazzle	twinkle	groove	gracious
glimpse	tremendous					

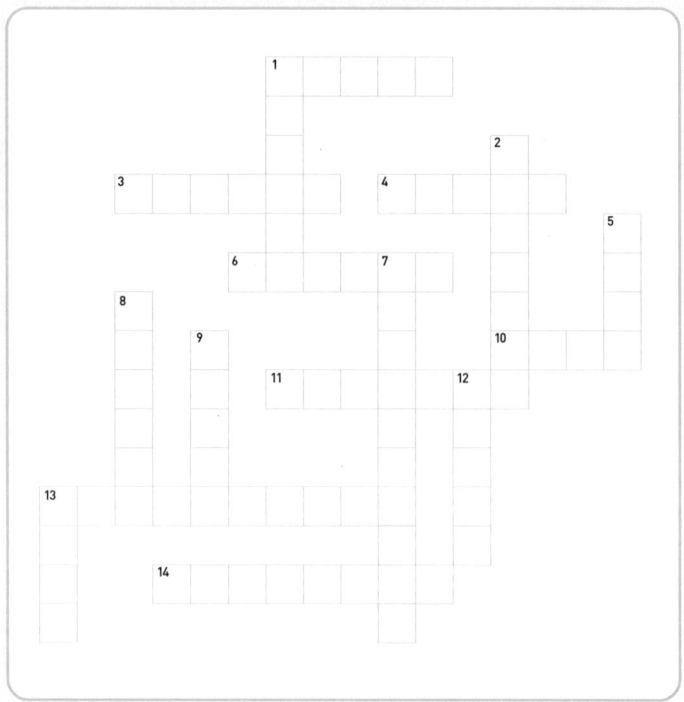

Chapter 6-10

Across

1 Unpleasantly wet and soft.
3 A long narrow hollow space cut into a surface.
4 To move slowly, especially with the body stretched out along the ground.
6 Clever, especially in a dishonest or secretive way.
10 To move the tongue across the surface of something.
11 If you get a _____ of something, you see them very briefly and not very well.
13 Extremely interested in something.
14 Behaving in a pleasant, polite, calm way.

Down

1 To shake slightly because you are cold or frightened.
2 To shine repeatedly strongly then weakly, as if flashing on and off very quickly.
5 A large thick piece, especially of food.
7 Very great in amount or level, or extremely good.
8 If light _____s you, it makes you unable to see for a short time.
9 To become larger and rounder than usual; to (cause to) increase in size or amount.
12 When people _____ somewhere, they move there in a large group.
13 To say something suddenly in an angry way.

Comprehension Quiz

1. Which creatures were not in the room?

A. A Grasshopper and a Ladybug

B. A Spider and a Silkworm

C. A Centipede and an Earthworm

D. A Beetle and a Cockroach

2. How big was the Old Green Grasshopper?

A. As big as a baseball

B. As big as a fox

C. As big as a large dog

D. As big as a cow

Chapter 11

3. How do the giant bugs feel? (two answers)

A. Hungry

B. Happy

C. Famished

D. Sleepy

4. What does James think the giant bugs want to eat?

A. The peach

B. James

C. The aunts

D. The sleeping Silkworm

5. Who noticed that James was scared?

A. The fatherly Grasshopper

B. The kind Ladybug

C. The naughty Centipede

D. The blind Worm

6. What did the Centipede ask James to do?

A. Scratch my back

B. Brush my teeth

C. Sing me a song

D. Take off my shoes

Comprehension Quiz

1. How many legs does the Centipede say that he has?

A. Two

B. Twenty two

C. Forty two

D. One hundred

2. Why does the Earthworm get angry at the Centipede?

A. He is jealous of the Centipede's many legs

B. He is blind

C. He has no legs

D. He does not like the Centipede

3. What do gardeners think of worms?

A. They are pests

B. They are slimy beasts

C. They are useful and much loved creatures

D. They are useful for fishing

4. How did the animals become so big?

A. They ate the magic peach

B. They swallowed little magic stones in the ground

C. They ate a lot of rice

D. They swallowed growth formula

Chapter 12

5. What does James not think of the Centipede?

A. He is a rascal

B. He is funny

C. He has too many shoes

D. It is good to hear him laughing

Comprehension Quiz

1. How long did it take for James to take off the Centipede's shoes?
A. It took ten minutes
B. It took two hours
C. It took all night
D. It took a very long time

2. Why did it take so long to take off the Centipede's shoes?
A. Because the shoes were big
B. Because the Centipede had one hundred feet
C. Because the shoes were tied in complicated knots
D. Because the shoes were too small for the Centipede's feet

3. Who was making the light in the room?
A. The Spider
B. The Silkworm
C. The Worm
D. The Glowworm

4. Why is the light still on?
A. The Glowworm always has her light on
B. The Glowworm went to sleep with the light on
C. The Glowworm forgets to turn off the light
D. The Glowworm can't hear

Chapter 13

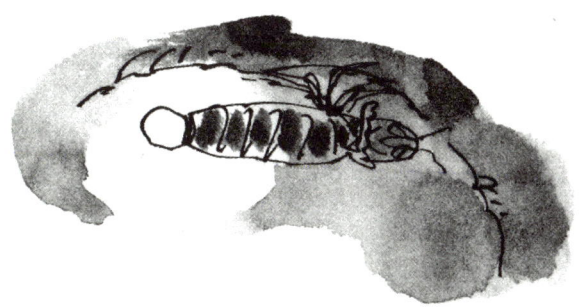

5. What did James think about his new friends?

A. They are scary and ugly

B. They are funny

C. They are kind and helpful

D. They are really terrible

Comprehension Quiz

1. Why are the insects going to cut the stem of the peach? (two answers)

A. So they can roll down the hill and get away from Spiker and Sponge
B. So Spiker and Sponge can no longer make any money from the peach
C. So they can go on a great adventure
D. So they can make peach juice

Chapter 14

2. Who cuts the peach stem?

A. The Old Green Grasshopper saws the stem with his legs

B. The Lightning bug burns away the stem with her lightning

C. The Spider poisons the stem with her venom

D. The Centipede nibbles away at the stem with his jaws

3. Which creatures will they not see?

A. A Creature with 49 heads and 49 noses to blow

B. A Pink Spotted Scrunch who eats people for lunch

C. A gnorrible Gnat that stings you from your knee to your hat

D. A Snozwangler that eats Oompa Loompas for every meal

4. What dangers will they face? (two answers)

A. An earthquake

B. A bomb

C. A virus

D. Frost

Comprehension Quiz

1. James did not come home last night. What do the Aunts think happened to James? (two answers)

A. He fell down a hole and broke his leg

B. He ran away

C. He met giant talking insects in the peach

D. He fell down a hole and broke his neck

Chapter 15

2. Why is Aunt Spiker angry at James?

A. Because he is injured

B. Because he will not be able to work for them

C. Because he did not obey

D. Because he has new friends

3. Put the events in order. (-   -   -   )

A. Aunt Spiker fell over Aunt sponge

B. Aunt Sponge tripped over the money box

C. They were as flat and thin and lifeless as paper dolls cut out of a picture book

D. They lay on the ground fighting and yelling

Build your Vocabulary

Chapter 11

- **frighten** [fráitn] *vt.* 놀라게 하다, 두려워하게 하다
  To make someone afraid.

- **recline** [rikláin] *vt.* 기대게 하다, 의지하다; *vi.* 기대다, 눕다
  To lean or lie back with the upper part of your body in a nearly horizontal position.

- **grasshopper** [grǽshɔ̀pər] *n.* [곤충] 메뚜기
  An insect with long back legs, that can jump very high and that makes a sound with its legs.

- **stool** [stu:l] *n.* 걸상
  A seat without any support for the back or arms.

- **enormous** [inɔ́:rməs] *a.* 막대한, 거대한
  Extremely large.

- **ladybug** [léidibʌ̀g] *n.* [곤충] 무당벌레
  A small red beetle which is round and has black spots.

- **scarlet** [skáːrlit] *n.* 주홍색, 진홍색; *a.* 주홍색[진홍색]의
  Bright red.

- **squat** [skwɑt] *vi.* 웅크리다, 쪼그리다; *a.* 웅크린, 쪼그린; 땅딸막한
  To position yourself close to the ground balancing on the front part of your feet with your legs bent under your body.

- **magnificent** [mægnífəsənt] *a.* 웅대한, 장엄한
  Very good, beautiful or deserving to be admired.

- **centipede** [séntəpìːd] *n.* [동물] 지네
  A small, long, thin animal with many legs.

- **earthworm** [ə́:rθwə̀:rm] *n.* 지렁이, 땅속에 사는 벌레
  A common type of worm, which moves through the earth.

- **behold** [bihóuld] *vt.* 보다
  If you behold someone or something, you see them.

- **famish** [fǽmiʃ] *vt.* 굶주리게 하다
  If you are famished, you are very hungry.

- **wriggle** [rígəl] *v.* 꿈틀거리다, 몸부림치다; *n.* 몸부림침, 꿈틀거림
  To twist your body, or move part of your body, with small, quick movements.

Chapter 11-15

- C **delicate** [délikət] *a.* 섬세한; 미묘한; 민감한; 허약한, 가냘픈
  Needing careful treatment, especially because easily damaged.

- C **shiver** [ʃívər] *v.* (추위·공포로) 후들후들 떨다
  To shake slightly because you are cold or frightened.

- **roar** [rɔːr] *vi.* 으르렁거리다, 고함치다, 외치다
  To make a long, loud, deep sound.

- **crew** [kruː] *n.* 승무원, 선원
  The people who work on and operate a ship or aircraft.

Chapter 12

- **disagreeable** [dìsəgríːəbəl] *a.* 불유쾌한, 싫은; 까다로운
  Unpleasant.

- **murmur** [mə́ːrmər] *v.* 중얼거리다
  To speak or say very quietly.

- **marvelous** [máːrvələs] *a.* 놀라운, 믿기 어려운; (구어) 훌륭한, 우수한
  Extremely good.

- **fellow** [félou] *n.* 친구, 동료, 사나이, 녀석
  People that you feel you have something in common with.

- **whisper** [hwíspər] *v.* 속삭이다, 소곤거리다; *n.* 속삭임
  To speak very quietly to somebody so that other people cannot hear what you are saying.

- M **splendid** [spléndid] *a.* 화려한, 멋진
  Very good.

- **slither** [slíðər] *vi.* 주르르 미끄러지다; 미끄러져 가다
  To move easily and quickly across a surface while twisting or curving.

- **prim** [prim] *a.* 꼼꼼한, 딱딱한; (특히 여자가) 새침 떠는
  Very formal and correct in behaviour and easily shocked by anything rude.

- **slimy** [sláimi] *a.* 진흙투성이의 끈적끈적한; 불쾌한, 더러운
  Be friendly and pleasant in an insincere way.

- **pest** [pest] *n.* 유해물, 골칫거리; 해충; 페스트(병)
  An insect or small animal which is harmful or which damages crops.

Build your Vocabulary

- **wither** [wíðər] *v.* 시들다, 말라죽다
  To become weak and dry and decay.

- **scornful** [skɔ́ːrnfəl] *a.* 경멸하는, 비웃는 (scornfully *ad.* 경멸적으로, 깔보면서)
  If you are scornful of someone or something, you show contempt for them.

- **colossal** [kəlásəl] *a.* 거대한, (구어) 어마어마한, 굉장한
  Extremely large.

- **peculiar** [pikjúːljər] *a.* 이상한, 별난; 특이한, 눈에 띄는
  Unusual and strange, sometimes in an unpleasant way.

- **swallow** [swálou] *v.* 삼키다, 들이켜다; *n.* 삼킴, 마심
  To make food, drink, etc. go down your throat into your stomach.

- **interrupt** [ìntərʌ́pt] *v.* 가로막다, 저지하다, 방해하다
  To say or do something that makes someone stop what they are saying or doing.

- **glee** [gliː] *n.* 기쁨, 즐거움
  Happiness, excitement or pleasure.

- **rascal** [rǽskəl] *n.* 악당, 깡패, 장난꾸러기, 녀석
  A person, especially a child or a man, who does things of which you disapprove, but whom you still like.

Chapter 13

- **thread** [θréd] *n.* 실; *v.* 실을 꿰다
  A thin string of cotton, wool, silk, etc. used for sewing or making cloth.

- **hammock** [hǽmək] *n.* 해먹 (달아매는 그물 침대)
  A type of bed used especially outside, consisting of a net or long piece of strong cloth which you tie between two trees or poles so that it swings.

- **magnificent** [mægnífəsənt] *a.* 웅대한, 장엄한
  Very good, beautiful or deserving to be admired.

- **shimmer** [ʃímər] *v.* 희미하게 반짝이다; *n.* 희미한 빛, 미광
  To shine in such a way that the light seems to shake slightly and quickly.

- **gossamer** [gásəmər] *n.* 잔 거미집; 얇은 천[실]; *a.* 잔 거미집 같은
  The very thin thread that spiders produce to make webs.

Chapter 11-15

for goodness' sake *idiom* 제발, 아무쪼록, 부디

frantically [fræntikəli] *ad.* 미친 듯이, 광포하게, 광란하여
Behaving in a wild and uncontrolled way.

knot [nɑt] *n.* 매듭, 매듭으로 만든 혹; *v.* 매듭을 짓다, 매다
A fastening made by tying together the ends of a piece or pieces of string, rope, cloth, etc.

amble [ǽmbəl] *v.* (사람이) 천천히 걷다
To walk in a slow and relaxed way.

coil [kɔil] *v.* 똘똘 감다, 사리다; *n.* 고리, 사리; [전기] 코일
To wind into a series of circles; to make something do this.

wheeze [hwi:z] *v.* 씨근거리다, 헐떡이며 말하다; *n.* (영·구어) 계략 계획
To make a high, rough noise while breathing because of some breathing difficulty.

crouch [krautʃ] *v.* 몸을 구부리다, 쭈그리다, 웅크리다
To bend your knees and lower yourself so that you are close to the ground and leaning forward slightly.

mumble [mʌ́mbəl] *v.* 중얼[웅얼]거리다; 우물우물 씹다; *n.* 중얼거림
To speak unclearly and quietly so that the words are difficult to understand.

glowworm [glóuwə̀:rm] *n.* (빛을 내는) 반딧불이의 유충; 날개 없는 반딧불이
A beetle, of which the females and young produce a green light from the tail.

stir [stə:r] *v.* 휘젓다, 움직이다, 흔들다; 흥분시키다
To mix a liquid or other substance by moving an object such as a spoon in a circular pattern.

hurl [hə:rl] *v.* 세게 내던지다, 집어던지다
To throw something with a lot of force.

Chapter 14

heave [hi:v] *vt.* (무거운 것을) 들어 올리다; *vi.* 올라가다, 높아지다
To move something heavy using a lot of effort.

leap [li:p] (leapt-leapt) *v.* 껑충 뛰다; 뛰어넘다; *n.* 뜀; 비약
To make a large jump or sudden movement, usually from one place to another.

Build your Vocabulary

- **depart** [dipá:rt] *v.* (열차·사람 등이) 출발하다, 떠나다; 벗어나다, 빗나가다
  To go away or leave, especially on a journey.

- **ghastly** [gǽstli] *a.* 핼쑥한, 송장 같은, 무서운
  Unpleasant and shocking.

- **desolate** [désəlit] *a.* 황폐한, 황량한, 쓸쓸한
  Unattractive and empty, with no people or nothing pleasant in it.

- **repulsive** [ripʌ́lsiv] *a.* 싫은, 불쾌한; 되쫓아버리는, 박차는; 쌀쌀한
  Extremely unpleasant or unacceptable.

- **lurch** [lə:rtʃ] *n.* (배·차 등의) 갑작스런 기울어짐; 비틀거림
  To make a sudden, unsteady movement forward or sideways.

- **nibble** [níbəl] *v.* 조금씩 물어뜯다, 갉아먹다; *n.* 조금씩 물어뜯기, 한 번 분량
  To eat something by taking a lot of small bites.

- **venomous** [vénəməs] *a.* 독액을 분비하는, 독이 있는; 해로운
  A poisonous liquid which some snakes, insects, etc. produce when biting or stinging.

- **scrunch** [skrʌntʃ] *vt.* 우두둑 깨물다; 우지끈 부수다; (언 눈 등을) 저벅저벅 밟다
  To crush material such as paper or cloth into a rough ball in the hand.

- **tuft** [tʌft] *n.* (머리칼·깃털·실 따위의) 술, 타래, 한 움큼
  A number of pieces of hair, grass, etc. growing or held closely together at the base.

- **biddy** [bídi] *n.* 암탉; 병아리; (수다스러운) 늙은 여인
  Hen.

- **well-bred** [wélbréd] *a.* 예의바른; 행실이 좋은, 점잖은
  Speaking or behaving in a way that is generally considered correct and polite.

- **blow off** *phrasal v.* …을 불어 날리다
  To remove or destroy something violently with an explosion.

- **gnu** [nju:] *n.* [동물] 누 (남아프리카 산의 암소 비슷한 영양)
  A large African animal with a long tail and horns that curve to the sides, which lives in areas covered with grass.

- **gnocerous** 번역서에는 gnu가 암소로, gnocerous는 수소로 번역되어 있다.

- **gnormous and gnorrible** 로알드 달이 라임을 맞추기 위해 만들어낸 수식어. 번역서에는 '엄청 크고 무서운(enormous and horrible)'으로 번역되어 있다.

Chapter 11-15

- **gnat** [næt] *n.* 피를 빨아 먹는 작은 곤충, 각다귀
  A very small flying insect that bites animals and people.

tremor [trémər] *n.* 약한 지진, 진동; 떨림, 전율
A small earthquake in which the ground shakes slightly.

- **plunge** [plʌndʒ] *vt.* 던져 넣다, 던지다, 찌르다; *vi.* 뛰어들다, 돌입하다, 잠수하다
  To move or make someone or something move suddenly forwards and/or downwards.

insidious [insídiəs] *a.* 교활한, 음흉한; 잠행성의
(insidiously *ad.* 교활하게, 음흉하게)
Gradually and secretly causing harm.

- **tilt** [tilt] *vi.* 기울이다, 뒤집다
  To (cause to) move into a sloping position.

Chapter 15

- **horrid** [hɔ́ːrid] *a.* 무시무시한; 매우 불쾌한, 지겨운
  Unpleasant or unkind.

good gracious *idiom* 이런!, 어머나!, 아뿔싸! (놀람의 소리)
Some people say good gracious or goodness gracious in order to express surprise or annoyance.

- **gape** [geip] *vi.* 입을 크게 벌리다; 멍청히 입을 벌리고 바라보다
  To look in great surprise at someone or something, especially with an open mouth.

- **panic** [pǽnik] *v.* (panicked-panicked) 당황하다, 허둥대다; *n.* 공황
  To feel so worried or frightened that you cannot think or behave calmly.

- **jostle** [dʒásl] *v.* 떠밀다, 부딪치다, 헤치고 나아가다; *n.* 혼잡; 부딪침
  To push roughly against someone in a crowd of people.

trip over *phrasal v.* 걸려 넘어지다, 걸려서 엎드러지다

iron out *phrasal v.* 다리미로 다리다; 롤러로 고르게 하다; 제거하다

Crossword Puzzle

Use the clues and the words in the box to complete the crossword puzzle.

tilt   jostle   shiver   wheeze   horrid   nibble   desolate
murmur   scarlet   mumble   wriggle   squat   splendid   frantically
colossal   enormous

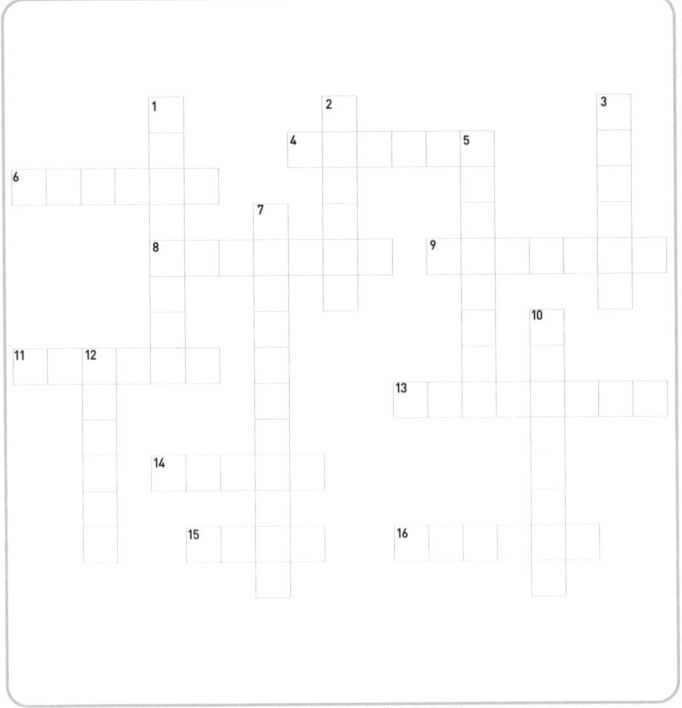

Chapter 11-15

Across

4   To make a high, rough noise while breathing because of some breathing difficulty.
6   To eat something by taking a lot of small bites.
8   Bright red.
9   To twist your body, or move part of your body, with small, quick movements.
11 To speak unclearly and quietly so that the words are difficult to understand.
13 Unattractive and empty, with no people or nothing pleasant in it.
14 To position yourself close to the ground balancing on the front part of your feet with your legs bent under your body.
15 To (cause to) move into a sloping position.
16 Unpleasant or unkind.

Down

1   Extremely large.
2   To shake slightly because you are cold or frightened.
3   To knock or push roughly against someone in order to move past them or get more space when you are in a crowd of people.
5   Extremely large.
7   Behaving in a wild and uncontrolled way.
10 Very good.
12 To speak or say very quietly.

Comprehension Quiz

1. What animals did the peach not hit?

A. A herd of cows

B. A flock of sheep

C. A bevy of geese

D. A yard of pigs

2. What building did the peach hit?

A. A post office

B. A police station

C. A bank

D. A chocolate factory

3. What happened to Daisy Entwistle?

A. Her shopping cart was flattened.

B. The skin on her nose was taken off

C. She lost her purse

D. She met a new friend

4. Where did the peach leave land for the sea?

A. At Spiker and Sponge's house

B. At the farmhouse which has a yard of pigs

C. In Seoul at the Han river

D. At Dover the most famous cliffs in England

Chapter 16

5. What is special about this part of the sea?

A. There are many rocks in the sea which destroy ships

B. There is a light house to protect the ships

C. There are sharks in the water

D. There are a lot of giant peaches in the water next to James

Comprehension Quiz

1. What did the insects do when the peach hit Spiker and Sponge?

A. They cried

B. They were silent

C. They smiled

D. They cheered

Chapter 17

2. What was not flying around the room?

A. A sofa

B. 21 pairs of boots

C. The light

D. The insects

3. How many times did James get tangled up in Spider's legs?

A. Once

B. Twice

C. Five times

D. Ten times

4. What happened when the Earthworm grabbed James?

A. He danced with James

B. He would not let go

C. He tickled James

D. He cracked himself like a whip

5. What did Spider do while the others were helping Centipede with his shoes?

A. She made a rope ladder

B. She made new beds

C. She opened the side door

D. She made a rope

Comprehension Quiz

1. Why did the insects panic when they saw that the giant peach was in the sea?

A. Because they were bobbing up and down
B. Because they thought they were sinking
C. Because they were floating beautifully
D. Because the waves were bibbling against the sides of the peach

2. What is the second reason to panic?

A. A storm is coming
B. The Earthworm likes to panic
C. There is nothing to eat
D. Sharks are eating the peach

Chapter 18

3. What is the Earthworm's final problem?

A. There is no problem

B. The peach is rolling

C. They will eat the peach and it will sink very soon

D. The birds will eat the peach and it will sink very soon

4. What did the Ladybug eat before tasting the peach?

A. A bluebottle in a spider web

B. Mosquitoes toes

C. Stinkbug eggs

D. Little green flies that live on rosebushes

5. What did the Centipede not eat?

A. Jellied Gnats

B. Earwigs

C. mudburgers

D. Bigfoot

Comprehension Quiz

1. What did the insects see in the water?

A. A pod of dolphins

B. A school of tuna

C. A group of sharks

D. A giant squid

2. Put the events in order. (　　-　　-　　-　　)

A. The insects panicked

B. The other sharks attacked the peach

C. The insects shouted "go away you filthy beast!"

D. The shark looked at the insects

Chapter 19

3. Why did the insects look a James for an idea to save them from the sharks?
A. Because James does not panic
B. Because James already had two good ideas
C. Because James is the oldest
D. Because James is the only boy

Comprehension Quiz

1. What is James' idea?

A. He will use skyhooks

B. He will use string to catch seagulls

C. He will use the power of his mind

D. He will make wings for the peach

2. What do "ridiculous, absurd, poppycock, and balderdash" mean?

A. Absolutely

B. Amusing

C. Uninteresting

D. Unbelievable

3. Where does the Old Green Grasshopper say the string can be found? (two answers)

A. The Silkworm

B. The peach

C. The Centipede's boots

D. The Spider

Chapter 20

4. What will the silk not be like?

A. As thick as your finger

B. As strong as you need

C. As black as night

D. As much as you need

5. How will James get the seagulls to come close to the peach?

A. He will use the Earthworm as bait

B. He will hypnotize the birds

C. He will use the peach as bait

D. He will shoot the birds with sticky spider silk and pull them in

• chapter 21. No Questions

Build your Vocabulary

Chapter 16

- **plunge** [plʌndʒ] *vt.* 던져 넣다, 던지다, 찌르다; *vi.* 뛰어들다, 돌입[잠수]하다
  To move or make someone or something move suddenly forwards and/or downwards.

- **hurtle** [hə́ːrtl] *vi.* 돌진하다, 고속으로 움직이다; 충돌하다
  To move very fast, especially in what seems a dangerous way.

- **telegraph pole** *n.* (영) 전신주, 전봇대
  Tall wooden pole used for carrying telephone or telegraph wires high above the ground.

- **madly** [mǽdli] *ad.* 미친 듯이, 미치광이처럼; (구어) 열광적으로, 필사적으로
  You can use madly to indicate that one person loves another a great deal.

- **herd** [həːrd] *n.* 짐승의 떼, (특히) 소, 돼지의 떼; 군중, 대중
  A large group of animals of the same type that live and feed together.

- **paddock** [pǽdək] *n.* 작은 방목장
  A small field where animals, especially horses, are kept.

- **seething** [síːðiŋ] *a.* 펄펄 끓는; 소용돌이치는; 들끓는
  To be full of a lot of people or animals, especially when they are all moving around.

- **stampede** [stæmpíːd] *v.* (가축 떼 등이) 놀라서 우르르 달아나다; *n.* 달아남
  When many large animals or many people suddenly all move quickly and in an uncontrolled way, usually in the same direction at the same time, especially because of fear.

- **gape** [geip] *vi.* 입을 크게 벌리다; 멍청히 입을 벌리고 바라보다
  To look in great surprise at someone or something, especially with an open mouth.

- **ooze** [uːz] *a.* 스며 나오다, 새어나오다 (oozy *a.* 스며 나오는, 새는)
  To flow slowly out of something through a small opening, or to slowly produce a thick sticky liquid.

- **wade** [weid] *vi.* (강 따위를) 걸어서 건너다; 힘들여 걷다, 고생하며 나아가다
  To walk with an effort through something, especially water or mud.

- **shriek** [ʃriːk] *n.* 날카로운 소리, 비명; *v.* 새된 소리로 말하다
  A short, loud, high cry.

Chapter 16-20

cowshed [káuʃèd] *n.* 외양간
A building where cows are kept while they are milked (= have milk taken from them), or where they are kept during winter or bad weather.

stable [stéibl] *a.* 안정된, 견고한; *n.* 마구간, 외양간
Firmly fixed or not likely to move or change.

pigsty [pígstài] *n.* 돼지우리, 누추한 집
A dirty or untidy place.

barn [bɑːrn] *n.* (농가의) 헛간, 광
A large building on a farm in which hay and grain are kept.

bungalow [bʌ́ŋgəlòu] *n.* 방갈로 (베란다가 붙은 간단한 목조 단층집)
A house that has only one storey.

hayrick [héirìk] *n.* (비에 젖지 않게 지붕을 해 씌운) 큰 건초 더미
A large pile of straw or hay that has been built in a regular shape.

topple [tápəl] *v.* 넘어지다, 쓰러지다
To (cause to) lose balance and fall down.

ninepin [náinpìn] *n.* 나인핀스(아홉개의 핀을 공을 굴려 쓰러뜨리는 실내경기)용 핀

whisk [hwisk] *v.* (먼지 등을) 털다, 털어내다; 휙 움직이다
To take something or someone somewhere else suddenly and quickly.

cliff [klif] 절벽, 낭떠러지
A high area of rock with a very steep side, often on a coast.

suspend [səspénd] *v.* 매달다, 걸다; 중지하다
To hang something from somewhere.

smack [smæk] *v.* 찰싹 치다; *n.* 찰싹 하는 소리
To hit something hard against something else so that it makes a short loud noise.

colossal [kəlásəl] *a.* 거대한, (구어) 어마어마한, 굉장한
Extremely large.

serene [sirí:n] *a.* 고요한, 잔잔한; 화창한, 청명한
Peaceful and calm; troubled by nothing.

Build your Vocabulary

Chapter 17

- **indescribable** [ìndiskráibəbəl] *a. n.* 형언할 수 없는; 말로 표현할 수 없는 [것]
  Impossible to describe, especially because of being extremely good or bad.

- **bruise** [bru:z] *v.* …에게 타박상을 주다, 멍들게 하다; *n.* 타박상, 멍
  An injury or mark where the skin has not been broken but is darker in colour, often as a result of being hit by something.

- **batter** [bǽtər] *v.* 연타하다, 쳐[때려]부수다, 쳐서 쭈그러뜨리다
  To hit and behave violently towards a person, especially a woman or child, repeatedly over a long period of time, or to hit something with force many times.

- **tangle** [tǽŋgəl] *n.* 엉킴, 얽힘; *vt.* 엉키게 하다, 얽히게 하다
  An untidy mass of things that are not in a state of order, or a state of confusion or difficulty.

- **tumble** [tʌ́mbəl] *v.* 넘어지다, 굴러 떨어지다
  To fall down quickly and suddenly, especially with a rolling movement.

- **burst** [bə́:rst] *n.* 폭발; 돌발; *v.* 파열하다, 터뜨리다
  A sudden, brief increase in something, or a short appearance of something.

- **flung** [flʌŋ] *v.* fling(던지다)의 과거, 과거 분사
  If you fling something somewhere, you throw it there using a lot of force.

- **fling up** *phrasal v.* 던져 올리다; 들어올리다

M - **rattle** [rǽtl] *v.* 덜걱덜걱 소리내다[움직이다]; *n.* 덜거덕거리는 소리
  To make a series of short loud sounds when hitting against something hard.

- **pea** [pi:] *n.* [식물] 완두(콩)
  A round green seed, several of which grow in a pod, eaten as a vegetable.

- **pitch** [pitʃ] *n.* 피치 (원유·콜타르 등을 증류시킨 뒤 남는 검은 찌꺼기), 송진
  (pitchy *a.* 까만, 캄캄한)
  A thick black substance which was used in the past to make wooden ships and buildings waterproof.

- **curse** [kə:rs] *vt.* 저주하다, 욕설을 퍼붓다; *n.* 저주, 악담
  To say a word or an expression which is not polite and shows that you are very angry.

- **horny** [hɔ́:rni] *a.* 뿔의, 뿔 모양의; 각질의
  Made of a hard substance, like horn.

Chapter 16-20

frantic [frǽntik] *a.* 광란의; 미친 사람 같은, 극도로 흥분한
Behaving in a wild and uncontrolled way.

disentangle [dìsentǽŋgl] *v.* (엉킨 것을) 풀다, 풀리다; 빠져나오다, 해방되다
To separate things that have become joined or confused.

glimmer [glímər] *vi.* 희미하게 빛나다; 깜빡이다
To shine with a weak light or a light that is not continuous.

take years off a person *idiom* 남을 나이보다 젊어지게 하다

bob up *phrasal v.* 불쑥 떠오르다[나타나다], 벌떡 일어서다
To move quickly in a particular direction.

giddy [gidi] *a.* 현기증 나는, 아찔한
If you feel giddy, you feel unsteady and think that you are about to fall over.

CM **for heaven's sake** *idiom* 제발, 아무쪼록, 부디

C **amidst** [əmìdst] (=amid) *prep* …의 한복판에, 한창 …하는 중에
In the middle of or surrounded by; among.

Chapter 18

bibble 사전에 없는 단어로 문맥 상 번역서에는 '출렁거리다[대다]' 로 번역되어 있다.

awkward [ɔ́:kwərd] *a.* 거북한, 어색한
An awkward situation is embarrassing and difficult to deal with.

C **perish** [périʃ] *v.* 멸망하다, 죽다, 썩어 없어지다; *n.* 궁핍 상태
To die, especially in an accident or by being killed, or to be destroyed.

C **wail** [wéil] *n.* 울부짖음, 비탄, 통곡; *vi.* 울부짖다
High-pitched mournful or complaining cry.

M **disaster** [dizǽstər] *n.* 재해, 참사
A very bad accident such as an earthquake or a plane crash.

M **odd** [ɑd] *a.* 이상한, 기묘한
Strange or unexpected.

C **golly** [gáli] *int.* (by-) 저런, 어머나, 아이고 (놀람·감탄)
Used to show surprise.

Build your Vocabulary

grisly [grizli] *a.* 섬뜩한, 소름끼치는
Extremely unpleasant, especially because death or blood is involved.

CM ★ **shrivel** [ʃríːvəl] *v.* 주름(살)지다[지게 하다], 줄어들다
To become or make something dry and wrinkled as a result of heat, cold or being old.

C ☆ **drown** [draun] *v.* 물에 빠져 죽다; 익사시키다
To die by being under water and unable to breathe, or to kill someone by causing this to happen.

rub it in *phrasal v.* (구어) (짓궂게) 되풀이하여 말하다, 상기시키다
If someone keeps reminding you of something you would rather forget you can say that they are rubbing it in.

jehoshaphat *n.* 여호사밧 (성경에 등장하는 유대국의 왕)

★ **affectionately** [əfékʃənətli] *ad.* 애정을 담고, 애정 어리게, 자애롭게
Showing feelings of liking or love.

★ **dent** [dent] *vt.* 움푹 들어가게 하다, 손상시키다
To make a small hollow mark in the surface of something.

★ **scoop** [skuːp] *vt.* 푸다, 뜨다, 퍼 올리다
To pick something up or remove it using a scoop or a spoon.

chunk [tʃʌŋk] *n.* 큰 덩어리; 상당한 양
A chunk of something is a large amount or large part of it.

CM ☆ **fabulous** [fǽbjələs] *a.* 굉장한, 멋진; 황당무계한, 믿어지지 않는
Very good; excellent.

☆ **prim** [prim] *a.* 꼼꼼한, 딱딱한; (특히 여자가) 새침 떠는, 점잔빼는
Very formal and correct in behaviour and easily shocked by anything rude.

rosebush [róuzbùʃ] *n.* 장미 관목[덩굴]

bluebottle [blúːbàtl] *n.* [식물] 수레국화; [곤충] 청파리
A big fly with a dark blue shiny body.

C **scrumptious** [skrʌ́mpʃəs] *a.* (구어) 몹시 즐거운, 멋진, 굉장한
If you describe food as scrumptious, you mean that it tastes extremely good.

Chapter 16-20

gnat [næt] *n.* 피를 빨아 먹는 작은 곤충, 각다귀
A very small flying insect that bites animals and people.

dandyprat 사전에 없는 단어로 번역서에는 '파리'로 번역되어 있다.

earwig [íərwìg] *n.* [곤충] 집게벌레
A small insect with two pincers at the back end of its body.

slime [slaim] *n.* (달팽이·물고기 등의) 점액; 끈적끈적한[찐득찐득한] 것; 진흙
A sticky liquid substance which is unpleasant to touch, such as the liquid produced by fish and snails and the greenish brown substance found near water.

sprinkle [spríŋkəl] *v.* (액체·분말 따위를) 뿌리다, 끼얹다, 붓다
To scatter a few bits or drops of something over a surface.

pinch [pintʃ] *v.* 꼬집다; 괴롭히다
To squeeze something, especially someone's skin, strongly between two hard things such as a finger and a thumb, usually causing pain.

grime [gráim] *n.* 때, 먼지, 검댕
A layer of dirt on skin or on a building.

dreg [dreg] *n.* (pl.) 잔재, 앙금; 하찮은 것, 쓰레기
If you talk about the dregs of society or of a community, you mean the people in it who you consider to be the most worthless and bad.

stinkbug [stíŋkbʌ́g] *n.* 악취를 풍기는 벌레; [곤충] 방귀벌레, 노린잿과의 곤충
stink [*v.* 악취를 풍기다] + bug [*n.* 벌레]

hornet [hɔ́ːrnit] *n.* ① 호박벌 ② 귀찮게 구는 사람, 심술쟁이; 곤란; 맹공격
A hornet is a large wasp.

tar [tɑːr] *n.* 타르; 콜타르 피치; (연기 속의) 진
One of the poisonous substances found in tobacco.

pail [peil] *n.* 들통, 물통; 양동이
A pail is a bucket, usually made of metal or wood.

snail [sneil] *n.* [동물] 달팽이, 늘보
A small creature with a soft wet body and a round shell, that moves very slowly and often eats garden plants.

beetle [bíːtl] *n.* [곤충] 딱정벌레, 갑충
An insect with a hard shell-like back.

Build your Vocabulary

vinegar [vínigər] *n.* 식초, 초
A sharp-tasting liquid, made especially from sour wine, malt or cider, which is used for flavouring or preserving food.

slobbage 사전에 없는 단어로 번역서에는 '데퉁바리'(말과 행동이 거칠고 미련한 사람)로 번역되어 있다.

mince [mins] *vt.* (고기 따위를) 다지다, 잘게 썰다; 조심스레 말하다
If you mince food such as meat, you put it into a machine which cuts it into very small pieces.

doodlebug [dúːdlbʌ̀g] *n.* 개미귀신 (명주잠자리과의 애벌레를 통틀어 이르는 말)
The larva of an ant lion or of any of several other insects.

slug [slʌg] *n.* [동물] 민달팽이
A small, usually black or brown, creature with a long soft body and no arms or legs, like a snail but with no shell.

wampfish 로알드 달이 만들어낸 생물. 번역서에는 '넙죽 생선'으로 번역되어 있다.

roe [róu] *n.* (물고기나 새우 등의) 알
Roe is the eggs or sperm of a fish, which is eaten as food.

pickle [píkəl] *v.* 소금물[식초]에 절이다; *n.* 절인 것
To preserve food in vinegar or salt water.

porcupine [pɔ́ːrkjəpàin] *n.* [동물] 호저 (부드러운 털과 뻣뻣한 가시털이 빽빽이 나 있으며 위험이 닥치면 몸을 밤송이처럼 동그랗게 한다)
An animal with a protective covering of long sharp quills.

tentacle [téntəkəl] *n.* (동물) 촉수, 더듬이
One of the long thin arm-like parts of some sea creatures.

octopus [áktəpəs] *n.* (pl.) [동물] 문어, 낙지
A sea creature with a soft oval body and eight tentacles.

poodle [púːdl] *n.* 푸들 (작고 영리한 북슬개)
A dog with curly hair that is usually cut short, except on its head, tail and legs.

armadillo [àːrmədílou] [동물] 아르마딜로 (남미 산의 야행성 포유동물)
A small animal whose body is covered in hard strips that allow it to curl into a ball when attacked.

mite [mait] *n.* ① 진드기 ② 적으나마 정성 어린 성금, 잔돈, 작은 것
A mite means to a small extent or degree.

C 빈출 **glint** [glint] *v.* 반짝이다, 빛나다; *n.* 반짝임, 섬광
To produce small bright flashes of light reflected from a surface.

Chapter 19

★ **peer** [piər] *v.* 자세히 들여다보다, 응시하다
To look closely or carefully at something, especially when you cannot see it clearly.

★ **cruise** [kru:z] *v.* 순항하다, 돌아다니다; *n.* 순항
A journey on a large ship for pleasure, during which you visit several places.

M 빈출 **filthy** [fílθi] *a.* 불결한, 더러운
Extremely or unpleasantly dirty.

빈출 **swallow** [swálou] *v.* 삼키다, 들이켜다; *n.* 삼킴, 마심
To make food, drink, etc. go down your throat into your stomach.

★ **perambulator** [pəræmbjəlèitər] *n.* 유모차
Pram, a vehicle for moving a baby around which consists of a small enclosed bed supported by a frame on four wheels.

M **lunge** [lʌndʒ] *v.* 찌르다, 돌진하다, 치다
To move forward suddenly and with force.

C **aghast** [əgǽst] *a.* 소스라치게, 놀라서, 겁이 나서
Suddenly filled with strong feelings of shock and anxiety.

C ★ **cluster** [klʌ́stər] *v.* 집중 발생하다; 밀집하다[시키다]; 떼 짓다[짓게 하다]
A cluster of people or things is a small group of them close together.

빈출 **churn** [tʃə:rn] *v.* 휘젓다; 괴롭히다, 고민하게 하다
If something churns water, mud, or dust, it moves it about violently.

C **pandemonium** [pæ̀ndəmóuniəm] *n.* 수라장, 대혼란(의 곳)
A situation in which there is a lot of noise and confusion because people are excited, angry or frightened.

C ★ **wring** [riŋ] *v.* 짜다, 비틀다; 몸부림치다
To hold something tightly with both hands and twist it by turning your hands in opposite directions.

Build your Vocabulary

pathetical [pəθétikəl] (=pathetic) *a.* 무감각한; 냉담한
Making you feel pity or sadness.

Chapter 20

longish [ló(:)ŋiʃ] *a.* 기름한, 길쭉한
Quite long.

thresh [θreʃ] *vt.* (곡식을) 타작하다; 때리다; (꼬리를) 흔들다
To remove the seeds of crop plants by hitting them, using either a machine or a hand tool.

★ **coax** [kouks] *vt.* 구슬려 …시키다, 어르다, 달래다
To persuade someone gently to do something or go somewhere, by being kind and patient, or by appearing to be.

skyhook [skáihùk] *n.* 스카이 훅 (항공기로부터 투하되는 물자의 감속을 위한 회전하는 날개)

★ **jeer** [dʒíər] *vi.* 조소하다, 야유하다; *n.* 조롱, 희롱
To laugh or shout insults at someone to show you have no respect for them.

C ‡ **absurd** [əbsə́:rd] *a.* 불합리한, 부조리한, 터무니없는
Ridiculous or unreasonable; foolish in an amusing way.

poppycock [pápikàk] *n.* 무의미, 허튼 소리, 난센스
Nonsense.

balderdash [bɔ́:ldərdæ̀ʃ] *n.* 같잖은[허튼] 소리
Nonsense; something that is stupid or not true.

off one's head *idiom* 정신이 나가서; 미쳐서; 몹시 흥분하여
If you say that someone is off their head, you think that their ideas or behaviour are very strange, foolish, or dangerous.

C **dotty** [dáti] *a.* (구어) 머리가 돈; 점이 많은
Slightly strange or mentally ill.

‡ **bait** [bèit] *v.* 미끼를 달다, 미끼로 꾀다; *n.* 미끼
A small amount of food on a hook or in a special device used to attract and catch a fish or animal.

Chapter 16-20

not give a hoot *idiom* 조금도 개의치 않다
If you say that you don't give a hoot about something, you are emphasizing that you do not care at all about it.

peck [pek] *v.* 쪼다, 쪼아 먹다
When a bird pecks, it bites, hits or picks up something small with its beak.

martyr [máːrtər] *n.* 순교자, 희생자; (병 따위에) 늘 고통 받는 사람
A person who suffers greatly or is killed because of their political or religious beliefs, and is often admired because of it.

Crossword Puzzle

Use the clues and the words in the box to complete the crossword puzzle.

filthy   glint   rattle   cluster   fabulous   smack   tangle   amidst
shrivel   colossal   gape   shriek   absurd   perish   disaster   plunge

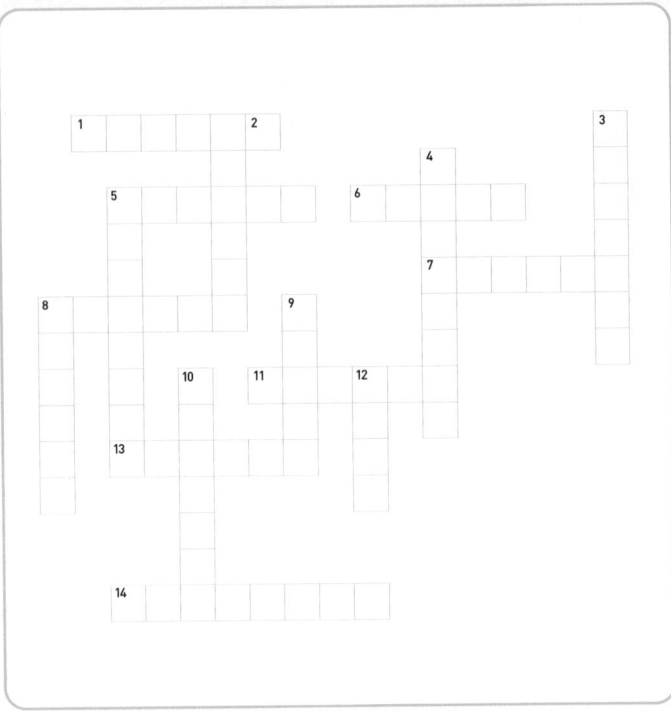

Across

1. Ridiculous or unreasonable; foolish in an amusing way.
5. Extremely or unpleasantly dirty.
6. To produce small bright flashes of light reflected from a surface.
7. In the middle of or surrounded by; among.
8. To (cause someone or something to) move or fall suddenly and often a long way forward, down or into something.
11. An untidy mass of things that are not in a state of order, or a state of confusion or difficulty.
13. A short, loud, high cry.
14. Extremely large.

Down

2. A short repeated sound, made when something shakes.
3. A cluster of people or things is a small group of them close together.
4. A very bad accident such as an earthquake or a plane crash.
5. Very good; excellent.
8. To die, especially in an accident or by being killed, or to be destroyed.
9. To hit something hard against something else so that it makes a short loud noise.
10. To become dry, smaller and covered with lines as if by crushing or folding, or to make something do this.
12. To look in great surprise at someone or something, especially with an open mouth.

Comprehension Quiz

1. Match the travelers to the job

A. James • • a. Bring the seagulls to the peach

B. Worm • • b. Spin the silk

C. Grasshopper and • • c. Catch the seagulls
Ladybug with the silk

D. Centipede • • d. Pull the worm away
from the seagulls

E. Silkworm and Spider • • e. Yell at the spinners

2. How much string did James pay out for each seagull?

A. 10 yards

B. 50 yards

C. 100 yards

D. 1 kilometer

Chapter 22

3. How many seagulls did the travelers catch?

A. 205

B. 308

C. 414

D. 502

4. What did the sharks do when the peach started lifting?

A. They went home

B. They attacked harder at the peach

C. The boiled the sea

D. The said "Hey, where are you going?"

Comprehension Quiz

1. When the peach rose which one did not happen?

A. The Earthworm did a wiggle of joy

B. The Grasshopper jumped higher and higher

C. The Spider ran in circles around the bottom of the peach

D. The Ladybug shook James' hand

2. Why did no one believe Miss Spider when she said that the bottom of the peach was not damaged? (two answers)

A. Because there were hundreds of sharks

B. Because sharks don't like insects

C. Because the sharks turned the sea to froth

D. Because the sharks opened their great gaping mouths

Chapter 23

3. Why couldn't the sharks bite the peach? (two answers)

A. They have long pointed noses

B. Their teeth are too big

C. The sharks blocked each other from eating

D. Their mouths are underneath their faces

4. What does the author compare the sharks and the peach to?

A. An alligator eating a turtle

B. A small dog biting a large ball

C. An elephant eating peanuts

D. A small dog biting a big dog

5. Why does the second officer think that the captain has been drinking whisky again?

A. Because the Captain is looking at a secret weapon

B. Because the Captain is using a telescope

C. Because the Captain is seeing a lot of birds

D. Because the Captain is seeing giant insects

Comprehension Quiz

1. What does the Old Green Grasshopper do?
A. He plays the drums with his feet
B. He beat boxes with his mouth
C. He plays the violin with his thigh and wing
D. He sings karaoke

2. How is the Old Green Grasshopper different from other grasshoppers?
A. He has ears on his knees
B. He has short horns
C. He has long horns
D. He uses only his wings to play music

3. What instrument does the Old Green Grasshopper say the long horns play?
A. The violin
B. The guitar
C. The ukulele
D. The banjo

Chapter 24

4. What animals have ears just below their knees?

A. Crickets and katydids

B. Snakes and worms

C. Ladybugs and aphids

D. Ants and termites

Comprehension Quiz

1. Why do farmers love earthworms? (two answers)

A. Because they are delicious

B. Because they change the color of the soil

C. Because they make the soil light and crumbly

D. Because they make things grow well

2. Why do farmers love ladybugs?

A. Because they tickle the farmers hand when they walk on it.

B. Because they eat all of the bugs that eat the farmers crops

C. Because they light up in the dark

D. Because they eat the farmers crops

3. What do the spots on a ladybug mean?

A. How old it is

B. How many bugs it eats

C. How pretty it is

D. What branch of the family it is from

Chapter 25

4. What happened to Miss Spider's father?

A. He was eaten by a bird

B. He had a fight with a centipede

C. He was washed down the bathtub drain by Aunt Sponge

D. He was smashed by Aunt Spiker

5. What is the superstition about killing a spider?

A. It is bad luck

B. Your hair will turn white

C. Your teeth will fall out

D. You will turn into a spider

Build your Vocabulary

Chapter 21

action stations *n.* [군사] 전투 배치
The positions to which soldiers go to be ready for fighting.

deck [dek] *n.* 갑판; 객차 지붕; 바닥
The top outside floor of a ship or boat.

c **scuttle** [skʌ́tl] *vi.* 급히 가다; 허둥지둥 도망가다; *n.* 종종걸음
To move quickly, with small short steps, especially in order to escape.

Chapter 22

dangle [dǽŋgəl] *v.* 매달리다[매달다], 흔들흔들 하다; *n.* 매달린 것
To hang loosely, or to hold something so that it hangs loosely.

CM **crouch** [kráutʃ] *v.* 몸을 구부리다, 쭈그리다, 웅크리다
To bend your knees and lower yourself so that you are close to the ground and leaning forward slightly.

c **hollow** [hálou] *a.* 속이 빈; 오목한, 움푹 팬; *v.* 속이 비다[비게 하다]
Having a hole or empty space inside.

exhort [igzɔ́ːrt] *vt.* 열심히 타이르다; 권고[충고·경고]하다
To strongly encourage or try to persuade someone to do something.

c **brute** [brúːt] *n.* 짐승, 야만인; *a.* 잔인한, 야만적인, 무정한
A rough and sometimes violent man.

swoop [swúːp] *v.* 내리 덮치다, 급강하하다
To move suddenly down through the air.

beak [bíːk] *n.* 새의 부리
The hard pointed part of a bird's mouth.

tug [tʌg] *vt.* 당기다, (세게) 잡아당기다; *n.* 힘껏 당김; 분투
To pull something quickly and usually with a lot of force.

tether [téðər] *vt.* 매다, 구속하다; *n.* 잡아매는 밧줄; 한계, 범위
To tie an animal to a post so that it cannot move very far.

prey [préi] *n.* 먹이; 희생양
An animal that is hunted and killed for food by another animal.

Chapter 21-25

- **hurl** [hə́:rl] *v.* 세게 내던지다, 집어던지다
  To throw something with a lot of force.

- **hover** [hʌ́vər] *v.* 하늘을 떠다니다, 비상하다
  To stay in one place in the air

- **sway** [swéi] *v.* 흔들다
  When people or things sway, they lean or swing slowly from one side to the other.

- **delicately** [délikətli] *ad.* 우아하게, 섬세하게; 미묘하게
  Needing careful treatment, especially because easily damaged.

- **harness** [há:rnis] *n.* 마구, 장치, 장비, 작업 설비
  A piece of equipment, with straps and fastenings, used to control or hold in place a person, animal or object.

- **majestical** [mədʒéstikəl] *a.* 위엄 있는, 당당한, 웅장한
  (majestically *ad.* 위엄 있게, 당당하게)
  Beautiful, powerful or causing great admiration and respect.

Chapter 23

- **squeal** [skwi:l] *v.* 깩깩거리다, 비명을 지르다
  If someone squeals, they make a long, high-pitched sound.

- **creep out** *phrasal v.* 몰래 기어나가다

- **wriggle** [ríɡəl] *v.* 꿈틀거리다, 몸부림치다; *n.* 몸부림침, 꿈틀거림
  To twist your body, or move part of your body, with small, quick movements.

- **steeple** [stí:pəl] *n.* (교회 등의) 뾰족탑, 첨탑; 첨탑 건물
  A pointed structure on the top of a church tower, or the tower and the pointed structure considered as one unit.

- **thread** [θréd] *n.* 실; *v.* 실을 꿰다
  To put something long and thin such as string or thread through a narrow hole or into a small space.

- **jiffy** [dʒífi] *n.* 잠시, 순간
  A very short time.

- **tuck** [tʌk] *v.* 밀어 넣다, 쑤셔 넣다
  To put or fold something into a small space.

Build your Vocabulary

- **clamber** [klǽmbər] *vi.* 기어 올라가다
  To climb up, across or into somewhere with difficulty, using the hands and the feet.

- **froth** [frɔ́:θ] *n.* 거품 *v.* 거품을 일으키다
  To have or produce a lot of small bubbles which often rise to the surface.

- **awkward** [ɔ́:kwərd] *a.* 거북한, 어색한 (awkwardly *ad.* 거북하게, 어색하게)
  An awkward situation is embarrassing and difficult to deal with.

- **funnel** [fʌ́nl] *n.* 깔때기; (깔때기꼴의) 환기통, 채광 구멍; 굴뚝
  An object which has a wide round opening at the top, sloping sides, and a narrow tube at the bottom, used for pouring liquids or powders into containers with narrow necks.

- **mutter** [mʌ́tər] *vi.* 중얼거리다, 낮게 투덜대다
  To speak quietly so that your voice is difficult to hear.

- **warn** [wɔːrn] *v.* 경고하다, 조심시키다; 예고하다
  To make someone aware of a possible danger or problem, especially one in the future.

- **teem** [tiːm] ① *vi.* 충만하다, 풍부하다, 비옥하다; ② *vt.* (그릇을) 비우다
  To contain large numbers of animals or people.

- **darn** [dɑːrn] ① *vt.* 감치다, 깁다, 꿰매다 ② (=damn) 혈뜯다; 저주하다
  Used instead of damn(=used to express anger or annoyance with someone or something) to express annoyance.

- **trousers** [tráuzərz] *n.* (pl.) (남자의) 바지
  A piece of clothing that covers the lower part of the body from the waist to the feet, consisting of two cylindrical parts, one for each leg, which are joined at the top.

Chapter 24

- **sway** [swéi] *v.* 흔들다
  When people or things sway, they lean or swing slowly from one side to the other.

- **spellbound** [spélbàund] *a.* 마법에 걸린, 넋을 잃은
  Extremely interested in something.

- **chirp** [tʃəːrp] *v.* 짹짹[찍찍] 울다[지저귀다]
  To make a short high sound or sounds.

- **chord** [kɔːrd] *n.* [음악] 화현, 화음; *v.* 가락이 맞다, 가락을 맞추다
  Three or more musical notes played at the same time.

Chapter 21-25

tune [tju:n] *n.* 곡조; 가락, 장단; 음조
A series of musical notes, especially one which is pleasant and easy to remember; a melody.

thigh [θái] *n.* 넓적다리
The part of a person's leg above the knee.

precisely [prisáisli] *ad.* 정밀하게, 정확히; 꼼꼼하게
Precisely means accurately and exactly.

feeler [fí:lər] *n.* [동물] 더듬이, 촉수
One of the two long parts on an insect's head with which it touches things in order to discover what is around it.

inferior [infíəriər] *a.* 보다 열등한, 하위의; *n.* 하급자, 열등한 사람
Not good, or not as good as someone or something else.

banjo [bǽndʒou] *n.* 밴조 (미국의 민속 음악이나 재즈에 쓰는 현악기)
A stringed musical instrument with a long neck and a hollow circular body.

fiddle [fídl] *n.* (구어) 바이올린; *vi.* 바이올린을 켜다, (손가락으로) 만지작거리다
A violin.

fascinate [fǽsənèit] *v.* 매혹하다, 꼼짝 못하게 하다; 마음을 끌다
To attract or interest somebody very much.

tummy [tʌ́mi] *n.* (유아어) 배 (stomach)
The stomach, or the lower front part of the body.

cricket [kríkit] *n.* 귀뚜라미
A brown or black insect which makes short loud noises by rubbing its wings together.

katydid [kéitidid] *n.* (미) 여치과(科)의 곤충

rambunctious [ræmbʌ́ŋkʃəs] *a.* 난폭한; 사나운; 제멋대로인
Full of energy and difficult to control.

Chapter 25

swallow [swálou] *v.* 삼키다, 들이켜다; *n.* 삼킴, 마심
To make food, drink, etc. go down your throat into your stomach.

Build your Vocabulary

- **crumbly** [krʌ́mbli] *a.* 부서지기 쉬운, 푸석푸석한
  Breaking easily into small pieces.

- **blush** [blʌʃ] *vi.* 얼굴을 붉히다
  To become red or pink in the face because of shame or joy.

- **sackful** [sǽkfùl] *n.* 부대 가득한 분량, 한 부대, 한 섬, 다량
  The amount contained in a sack.

- **gobble** [gábəl] *vt.* 게걸스레 먹다; 꿀떡 삼키다
  To eat food too fast.

- **scarlet** [skáːrlit] *n.* 주홍색, 진홍색; *a.* 주홍색[진홍색]의
  Bright red.

- **trifle** [tráifəl] *n.* 하찮은 것, 사소한 일; 조금, 약간
  A matter or item of little value or importance.

- **saucy** [sɔ́ːsi] *a.* 뻔뻔스런, 건방진; 쾌활한, 재치 있는
  Rude and lacking respect, or referring to sex, especially in a humorous way.

- **plug hole** [plʌ́ghóul] *n.* (영) (욕조·싱크대 등의) 마개 구멍
  A plughole is a small hole in a bath or sink which allows the water to flow away and into which you can put a plug.

- **ghastly** [gǽstli] *a.* 핼쑥한, 송장 같은, 무서운
  Unpleasant and shocking.

- **flabby** [flǽbi] *a.* (몸에 살이 쪄서) 흐느적흐느적한, 축 늘어진
  Soft and fat, weak.

- **soggy** [sági] *a.* 물에 잠긴, 흠빡 젖은
  Unpleasantly wet and soft.

- **paste** [peist] *n.* (붙이는) 풀, 밀가루 반죽
  A soft wet mixture, usually made of a powder and a liquid.

- **sleek** [sliːk] *a.* 윤기 있는, 매끄러운
  Smooth, soft and glossy.

- **frown** [fraun] *v.* 눈살을 찌푸리다, 얼굴을 찡그리다
  When someone frowns, their eyebrows become drawn together, because they are annoyed, worried, or puzzled.

Chapter 21-25

choc [tʃɑk] *n.* (구어) 초콜릿; 초콜릿 음료, 코코아
Chocolate.

CM복습 **bulge** [bʌ́ldʒ] *vi.* 부풀다, 불룩해지다, 부풀리다
To stick out in a round shape.

snigger [snígər] (=snicker) *vi.* 낄낄 웃다, 숨죽여 웃다
To laugh at someone or something childishly and often unkindly.

★ **swine** [swáin] *n.* (집합적) 돼지; 비열한 놈, 욕심쟁이
A person whom you consider to be extremely unpleasant and unkind.

★ **snuff** [snʌf] *n.* 냄새, 향기; 코담배; *v.* 코로 들이쉬다, 흥흥거리며 냄새를 맡다
Tobacco in the form of a powder for breathing into the nose.

※ **fiery** [fáiəri] *a.* 불의, 화염의; 불같은
Bright red, like fire.

tapioca [tæpióukə] *n.* 타피오카 (카사바(남아메리카가 원산지인 낙엽관목)의 뿌리로 만든 식용 전분)
Small hard pieces of the dried and crushed root of the cassava plant, usually cooked with milk and sugar to make a sweet food.

Mother Hubbard *n.* 허버드 아주머니 (영국 동요의 제목 및 그 여주인공)

Crossword Puzzle

Use the clues and the words in the box to complete the crossword puzzle.

froth	thigh	fiddle	crouch	hurl	frown	spellbound
bulge	wriggle	gobble	jiffy	flabby	scuttle	hollow
ghastly	thread					

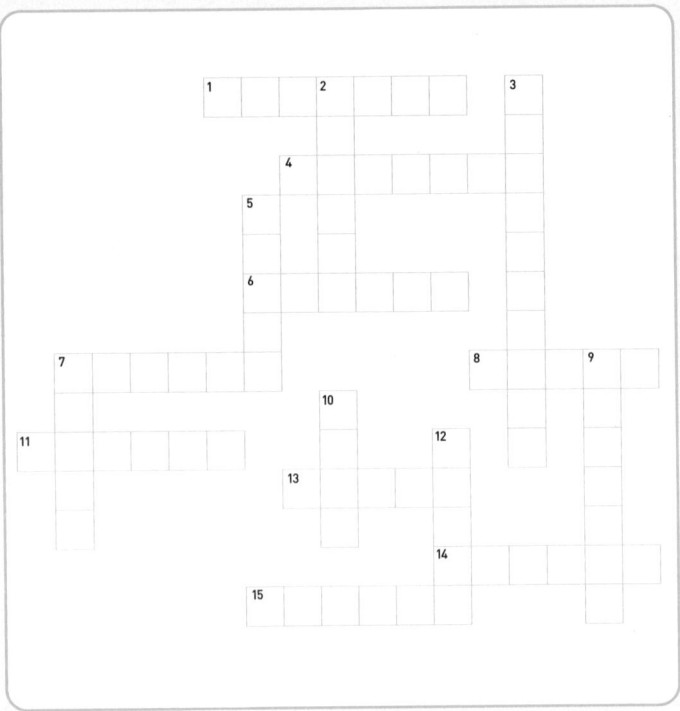

Across

1 To move quickly, with small short steps, especially in order to escape.
4 To twist your body, or move part of your body, with small, quick movements.
6 A violin.
7 Soft and fat, weak.
8 To stick out in a round shape.
11 Having a hole or empty space inside.
13 To have or produce a lot of small bubbles which often rise to the surface.
14 To eat food too fast.
15 To bend your knees and lower yourself so that you are close to the ground and leaning forward slightly.

Down

2 To put something long and thin such as string or thread through a narrow hole or into a small space.
3 Extremely interested in something.
5 A very short time.
7 When someone _____s, their eyebrows become drawn together, because they are annoyed, worried, or puzzled.
9 Unpleasant and shocking.
10 To throw something with a lot of force.
12 The part of a person's leg above the knee.

Comprehension Quiz

1. Why did the Centipede fall over the side of the peach?

A. He was looking over the edge

B. He was dancing too close to the edge

C. He was dizzy

D. He thought he could fly

2. What did James not do?

A. He told the Silkworm to start spinning

B. He tied the silk around his waist

C. He went bungee jumping

D. He tugged on the rope three times

3. What song did the Old Green Grasshopper play?

A. Ten minutes

B. Edelweiss

C. Four seasons

D. Funeral March

Chapter 26

4. How long was the string? (two answers)

A. One hundred meters

B. One kilometer

C. One mile

D. 1.6 kilometers

5. How did James save the Centipede?

A. He swam around in the ocean until he found the Centipede

B. He made a phone call on the way down

C. He fell into a boat which helped him search for the Centipede

D. He caught the Centipede on the way down

Comprehension Quiz

1. What do "Cloud-Men" not look like?

A. Tall wispy wraithlike

B. White

C. Cotton, candy floss, thin white hairs

D. Photocopy paper

2. Why can't people in airplanes see the Cloud-Men? (two answers)

A. Because airplanes are too fast

B. Because airplanes are too noisy

C. Because airplanes have small windows

D. Because airplanes are silver

3. What were the Cloud-Men making when the peach was flying by?

A. They were making snow balls for a fight

B. They were making hailstones as practice for winter

C. They were making cloud candy for Valentine's Day

D. They were making cloud marbles for a game

Chapter 27

4. Put the events in order: What happened after the Centipede yelled and gestured at the Cloud-Men? (-   -   -   )

A. They dropped their shovels and stared in surprise

B. They jumped around and gave a yelp of surprise

C. They threw the hailstones at the peach

D. They became infuriated beyond belief

5. How do the Cloud-Men throw the hailstones?

A. Whizzing through the air like bullets from a machine gun

B. Softly falling like snow

C. Bouncing like a ball

D. Exploding like a bomb

6. Who got hit by a hailstone? (two answers)

A. James

B. The Centipede

C. The Ladybug

D. The Old Green Grasshopper

Comprehension Quiz

1. What did the animals not think the Cloud-Men were making?

A. A bridge

B. A hoop cut in half

C. An upside down horseshoe

D. An arch

2. What would the Old Green Grasshopper rather do than fighting the Cloud-Men again?

A. Be on the end of a fish hook

B. Be fried alive and eaten

C. Jump off of the peach and fall in the ocean

D. Be stuck in a spider web

3. How were the Cloud-Men going to lower the rainbow when it was finished?

A. They used seagulls to fly it down

B. They used airplanes to fly it down

C. They used ropes to lower it

D. They used the wind to lower it

Chapter 28

4. Put the events in order: What happened when the peach broke the rainbow? (-   -   -   )

A. The Cloud-Men let go of the ropes

B. One tall Cloud man jumped over to the peach

C. The Centipede cut the string

D. The seagull carried the Cloud Man away

5. What did the Cloud-Men not throw at the peach?

A. Paint pots

B. Step ladders

C. Hair oil

D. Hail stones

Comprehension Quiz

1. What is special about rainbow paint?

A. It dries very hard and fast

B. There are eight different colors

C. It tastes like grapes

D. It is used for making statues

2. Why is Miss Spider afraid of paint? (two answers)

A. Because she can't paint well

B. Because her mother fed her grandmother

C. Because her grandmother was stuck in paint for six months

D. Because Aunt sponge killed her grandmother with a mop

Chapter 29

3. What ideas did the animals have for removing the paint from Centipede? (two answers)

A. Use sandpaper
B. Put a bird-bath on his head
C. Wash him off
D. Pull him out by his tongue

Comprehension Quiz

1. What did the cloud look like?

A. It looked like cotton candy

B. It looked like Cloud-men holding hands

C. It looked like a giant black dangerous thundery cloud

D. It looked like a tornado

2. What did the Cloud-Man say?

A. Let them have it

B. Drown them

C. Remember the rainbow

D. On with the faucets

3. What did the cloud look like when it opened up?

A. Like a zipper on a backpack

B. Like laces on a shoe

C. Like a paper bag splitting open

D. Like a balloon popping

Chapter 30

4. What was the cloud not compared to?

A. A lake

B. An ocean

C. A waterfall

D. A lagoon

5. What did the Centipede say after passing the rain cloud?

A. I am drowned

B. I am full of water

C. I am free

D. I am still a statue

Build your Vocabulary

Chapter 26

- **teeter** [tíːtər] v. 흔들리다, 비틀거리며 나가다
  To appear to be about to fall while moving or standing.

- **brink** [briŋk] n. (벼랑의) 가장자리, 물가; 직전
  The point where a new or different situation is about to begin.

- **frantic** [frǽntik] a. 광란의, 미친 듯 날뛰는 (frantically ad. 미친 듯이)
  Behaving in a wild and uncontrolled way.

- **tumble** [tʌ́mbəl] v. 넘어지다, 굴러 떨어지다
  To fall down quickly and suddenly, especially with a rolling movement.

- **haul** [hɔ́ːl] vt. 세게 잡아끌다, 끌어당기다, 운반하다; n. 견인, 운반
  To pull something heavy slowly and with difficulty.

- **sob** [sɔ́b] vi. 흐느껴 울다
  To cry noisily, taking in deep breaths.

- **tug** [tʌg] n. 힘껏 당김; 분투; vt. 당기다, (세게) 잡아당기다
  To pull something quickly and usually with a lot of force.

- **be dripping-wet** idiom 흠뻑 젖어 있다

- **gasp** [gǽsp] v. 헐떡거리다; 숨이 막히다; n. 헐떡거림
  To take a short quick breath through the mouth, especially because of surprise, pain or shock.

- **pat** [pǽt] v. 가볍게 두드리다
  To touch someone or something gently.

Chapter 27

- **crouch** [kráutʃ] v. 몸을 구부리다, 쭈그리다, 웅크리다
  To bend your knees and lower yourself so that you are close to the ground and leaning forward slightly.

- **menace** [ménəs] n. (구어) 골칫거리, 말썽꾸러기; 협박, 공갈
  Something or someone that is very annoying or troublesome.

- **eerie** [íəri] a. 섬뜩한, 무시무시한, 기분 나쁜, 기괴한
  Strange in a frightening and mysterious way.

Chapter 26-30

sway [swéi] *v.* 흔들다
When people or things sway, they lean or swing slowly from one side to the other.

flock [flɑk] *n.* (양·새·사람 등의) 떼, 무리, 다수; *v.* 모이다
A group of sheep, goats or birds of the same type.

clatter [klǽtər] *n.* (식기류 따위의) 덜걱덜걱 하는 소리; *v.* 달가닥달가닥 울리다
To make continuous loud noises by hitting hard objects against each other, or to cause objects to do this.

lurk [lə́ːrk] *v.* 숨다, 잠복하다; *n.* 잠복, 밀행
To wait or move in a secret way so that you cannot be seen, especially because you are about to attack someone or do something wrong.

stealthy [stélθi] *a.* 남의 눈을 피하는, 몰래 하는, 비밀의
(stealthily *ad.* 몰래, 은밀히)
Doing things quietly or secretly; done quietly or secretly.

wraith [réiθ] *n.* 생령, 망령, 유령 (wraithlike *a.* 생령 같은, 유령 같은)
A wraith is a ghost.

candy-floss *n.* (영) 솜사탕; 겉보기만 그럴듯한 것
A large soft ball of white or pink sugar in the form of thin threads, which is usually sold on a stick and eaten at fairs and amusement parks.

huddle [hʌ́dl] *v.* 붐비다, (떼 지어) 몰리다, 쌓아 올리다
To heap or crowd together closely.

stammer [stǽmər] *v.* 말을 더듬다, 더듬으며 말하다
To speak or say something with unusual pauses or repeated sounds, either because of speech problems or because of fear and anxiety.

salami [səlɑ́ːmi] *n.* 살라미 소시지 (향미가 강한 이탈리아 소시지)

quiver [kwívər] *vi.* 떨리다, 흔들리다
To shake slightly, often because of strong emotion.

peculiar [pikjúːljər] *a.* 이상한, 별난; 특이한, 눈에 띄는
Unusual and strange, sometimes in an unpleasant way.

marble [mɑ́ːrbəl] *n.* 대리석; (pl.) (속어) 정상의 판단력, 분별
A type of very hard rock which has a pattern of lines going through it, feels cold and becomes smooth and shiny when cut and polished.

Build your Vocabulary

wispy [wíspi] *a.* 가늘고 연약한, 희미한, 약간의
Consisting of small, thin pieces; not thick.

c ‡ **shovel** [ʃʌ́vəl] *n.* 삽
A tool with a rounded blade and a long handle used for moving sand, stones or snow.

c ★ **whoop** [húː(ː)p] *v.* 고함지르다, 큰 소리로 말하다; *n.* 함성
To give a loud, excited shout, especially to show your enjoyment of or agreement with something.

CM ★ **chant** [tʃænt] *v.* 일제히 외치다; (노래를) 부르다
To repeat of sing a religious prayer or song to a simple tune.

‡ **hail** [héil] ① *n.* 싸락눈, 우박; *vi.* 우박이 내리다 ② *vt.* 환영하다
Hail consists of small balls of ice that fall like rain from the sky.

hailstone [héilstòun] *n.* 싸락눈, 우박
A small hard ball of ice which falls from the sky like rain; a piece of hail.

imbecile [ímbəsil] *a.* 저능한, 우둔한, 천치의
A person who behaves in a stupid way.

★ **knob** [nɑb] *n.* (문·서랍 등의 둥근) 손잡이; 혹, 마디
A round handle, or a small round device for controlling a machine or electrical equipment.

c **nincompoop** [nínkəmpùːp] *n.* 바보, 멍청이
A foolish or stupid person.

half-wit [hǽfwìt] *n.* 얼빠진 놈, 반편; 정신박약자
A stupid person.

★ **blunder** [blʌ́ndər] *n.* 큰 실수; *v.* 큰 실수를 하다, 일을 그르치다; 무심코 말하다
A big mistake, usually caused by lack of care or thought.

ass [æs] *n.* (경멸) 개자식; (비어) 엉덩이; 항문
A stupid person.

CM ‡ **wasp** [wɑsp] *n.* 장수말벌; 성질 잘 내는 사람

★ **yelp** [jelp] *n.* 소리침, 비명; (개 따위의) 캥캥 짖는 소리
To make a sudden, short, high sound, usually when in pain.

★ **loathsome** [lóuðsəm] *a.* 싫은, 지긋지긋한; 불쾌한, 역겨운
Extremely unpleasant.

Chapter 26-30

M **infuriate** [infjúərièit] *v.* 격노케 하다
To make someone extremely angry.

: **lump** [lʌmp] *n.* 덩어리, 덩이; *v.* 덩어리로 만들다
A piece of a solid substance, usually with no particular shape.

: **lead** [li:d] ① *n.* [광물] 납 ② *v.* 인도하다, 선두에 서다
A heavy soft grey metal, used especially in the past for water pipes or to cover roofs.

C **whiz[z]** [hwiz] *v.* 씽[윙] 소리나다[하며 움직이다]
To move very quickly, making a high continuous sound.

M **squelch** [skweltʃ] *v.* 짓누르다, 찌부러뜨리다; *n.* 찌부러뜨림
To stop something from growing, increasing or developing.

cannonball [kǽnənbɔ̀:l] *n.* 포탄; *a.* 굉장히 빠른
A large metal or stone ball that is fired from a cannon.

M : **wreck** [rek] *v.* 파괴하다, 부수다, 난파시키다; *n.* 난파, 파선, 조난
To destroy or badly damage something.

Chapter 28

복습 **shimmer** [ʃímər] *vi.* 희미하게 반짝이다; *n.* 희미한 빛, 미광
To shine in such a way that the light seems to shake slightly and quickly.

복습 **peer** [piər] *v.* 자세히 들여다보다, 응시하다
To look closely or carefully at something, especially when you cannot see it clearly.

horseshoe [hɔ́:rsʃù:] *n.* 편자 (말굽에 붙이는 U모양 쇳조각)
A U-shaped piece of metal which is fixed to the bottom of a horse's hoof to protect it.

복습 **wail** [wéil] *n.* 울부짖음, 비탄, 통곡; *vi.* 울부짖다
To cry or complain about something in a loud high voice.

C 복습 **swarm** [swɔ:rm] *vi.* 떼를 짓다; *n.* 떼, 무리
When people swarm somewhere, they move there in a large group.

frenzy [frénzi] *n.* 격분, 격앙, 광란
Uncontrolled and excited behaviour or emotion.

Build your Vocabulary

- **enthrall** [enθrɔ́:l] *vt.* 매혹하다, 마음을 빼앗다, 사로잡다
  To keep someone completely interested.

- **wring** [riŋ] *v.* 짜다; 비틀다; 괴로워하다
  To hold something tightly with both hands and twist it by turning your hands in opposite directions.

- **tremendous** [triméndəs] *a.* 거대한, 대단한; 엄청난, 무서운
  Very great in amount or level, or extremely good.

- **thud** [θʌd] *n.* 퍽, 털썩, 쿵 (소리); 쾅 하고 침
  The sound that is made when something heavy falls or hits something else.

- **splinter** [splíntər] *v.* 쪼개[찢어]지다, 산산조각이 되다; *n.* 부서진 조각; *a.* 분리한
  A small sharp broken piece of wood, glass, plastic or similar material.

- **tangle** [tǽŋgəl] *n.* 엉킴, 얽힘; *vt.* 엉키게 하다, 얽히게 하다
  An untidy mass of things that are not in a state of order, or a state of confusion or difficulty.

- **pandemonium** [pæ̀ndəmóuniəm] *n.* 수라장, 대혼란(의 곳)
  A situation in which there is a lot of noise and confusion because people are excited, angry or frightened.

- **malevolent** [məlévələnt] *a.* 악의 있는; 남의 불행을 기뻐하는
  (malevolently *ad.* 악의로, 심술궂게)
  Causing or wanting to cause harm or evil.

- **cling** [kliŋ] *vi.* 달라붙다, 매달리다
  If you cling to someone or something, you hold onto them tightly.

- **mercy** [mə́:rsi] *n.* 자비, 연민
  Kindness and forgiveness shown towards someone whom you have authority over.

- **kipper** [kípər] *n.* 산란기(후)의 연어[송어] 수컷; 훈제 청어
  A herring that has been preserved by being treated with salt and then with smoke.

- **moonlit** [mú:nlit] *a.* 달빛에 비친, 달빛을 받은
  The pale light of the moon.

- **flabbergast** [flǽbərgæ̀st] *vt.* (구어) 소스라쳐 놀라게 하다, 당황하게 하다
  To shock someone, usually by telling them something they were not expecting.

Chapter 26-30

halve [hæv] *v.* 이등분하다; 반감하다
Either of the two equal or nearly equal parts that together make up a whole.

tumble [tʌ́mbəl] *v.* 넘어지다, 굴러 떨어지다
To fall down quickly and suddenly, especially with a rolling movement.

infuriate [infjúərièit] *v.* 격노케 하다
To make someone extremely angry.

pelt [pelt] *v.* 내던지다, 연타하다, 퍼붓다
To throw a number of things quickly at someone or something.

stepladder [stéplæ̀dər] *n.* 발판 사다리, 접사다리
A short, folding platform with steps.

dodge [dɑ́dʒ] *v.* 홱 피하다, 날쌔게 비키다
To avoid being hit by something by moving quickly to one side.

moan [móun] *v.* 신음하다, 끙끙대다
To make a long low sound of pain, suffering or another strong emotion.

Chapter 29

wretch [retʃ] *n.* 가련한[비참한] 사람; 철면피, 비열한 사람
Someone who is unpleasant or annoying.

encase [enkéis] *v.* (상자 등에) 넣다; 싸다
To cover or enclose something or someone completely.

rod [rɑd] *n.* 막대기, 지팡이; 작은 가지
A long straight piece of wood, metal or glass.

gurgle [gə́ːrgəl] *v.* (물 따위가) 콸콸 소리 내다, 콸콸 흐르다
If water is gurgling, it is making a bubbling noise when flowing.

detest [ditést] *v.* 몹시 싫어하다, 혐오하다
To hate someone or something very much.

fetch [fetʃ] *v.* (가서) 가져오다, 데려오다, 불러오다
To go to another place to get something or someone and bring them back.

lawn [lɔːn] *n.* 잔디, 잔디밭
An area of grass, especially near to a house or in a park, which is cut regularly to keep it short.

Build your Vocabulary

bird-bath [bə́:rd bǽθ] *n.* 새들이 목욕할 수 있는 물통

Chapter 30

swirl [swə:rl] *vi.* 빙빙 돌다
To move round and round quickly.

immense [iméns] *a.* 막대한, 무한한, 광대한
Extremely large in size or degree.

rumble [rʌ́mbəl] *v.* 우르르 울리다; 우르르 소리나게 하다
To make a long deep sound or series of sounds.

faucet [fɔ́:sit] *n.* 물 꼭지, 물 주둥이
A device that controls the flow of liquid, especially water, from a pipe.

grope [gróup] *v.* 손으로 더듬다[더듬어 찾다]; (비밀 등을) 찾다, 캐다
To feel with your hands, especially in order to find or move towards something when you cannot see easily.

slosh [slaʃ] *n.* (액체가) 튀어 흩어짐, 튀어 오름; *v.* 절벅절벅 휘젓다, 물을 튀기다
To move around making a lot of noise or coming out over the edge of something.

swash [swaʃ] *v.* 풍덩 소리 나다; 물을 튀기다; (세차게) 부딪치다

surge [sə:rdʒ] *v.* 파도처럼 밀려오다; *n.* 큰 물결, 쇄도
To move quickly and with force in a particular direction.

whirl [hwə:rl] *v.* 빙글 돌다, 선회하다
Move around or turn around very quickly.

gush [gʌʃ] *vi.* 세차게 흘러나오다, 분출하다; *n.* 분출, 솟아나옴
To flow or send out quickly and in large amounts.

deluge [délju:dʒ] *n.* 대홍수, 범람; 호우
A very large amount of rain or water.

somersault [sʌ́mərsɔ̀:lt] *n.* 재주넘기, 공중제비
A rolling movement or jump, either forwards or backwards, in which you turn over completely, with your body above your head, and finish with your head on top again.

hooray [hu(:)réi] (=hurrah) *int., n., vi.* 만세(를 부르다)
Used to express excitement, pleasure or approval.

Chapter 26-30

bruise [brúːz] *v.* …에게 타박상을 주다, 멍들게 하다; *n.* 타박상, 멍
An injury or mark where the skin has not been broken but is darker in colour, often as a result of being hit by something.

gent [dʒent] *n.* (구어) 신사; 신사인 체하는 사람
Polite man who behaves well towards other people, especially women.

Crossword Puzzle

Use the clues and the words in the box to complete the crossword puzzle.

whirl	frantic	quiver	slosh	sway	fetch	tumble	shimmer
huddle	squelch	swarm	chant	crouch	infuriate	stammer	

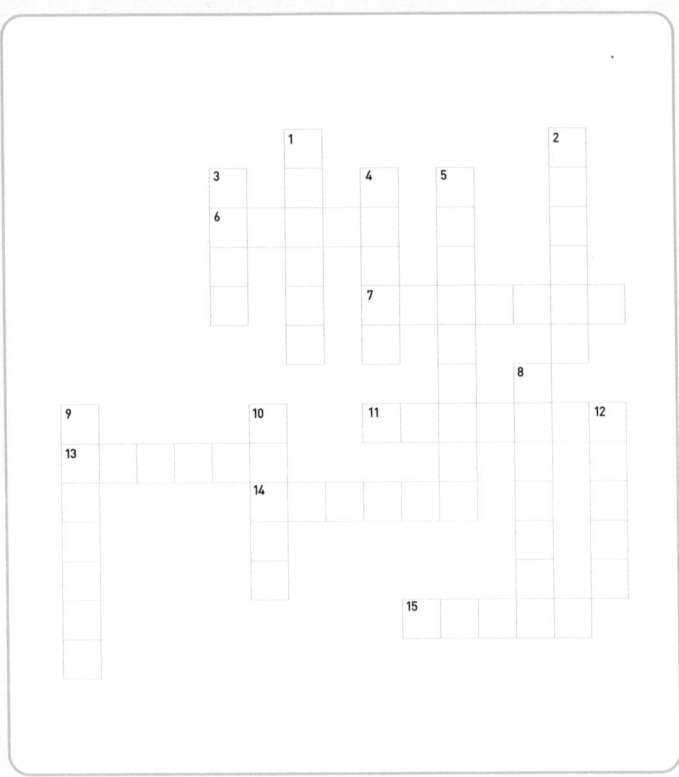

Chapter 26-30

Across

6   Move around or turn around very quickly.
7   Make a sucking sound like the one produced when you are walking on soft wet ground.
11 Behaving in a wild and uncontrolled way.
13 To heap or crowd together closely.
14 To fall down quickly and suddenly, especially with a rolling movement.
15 When people _____ somewhere, they move there in a large group.

Down

1   To shake slightly, often because of strong emotion.
2   To bend your knees and lower yourself so that you are close to the ground and leaning forward slightly.
3   When people or things _____, they lean or swing slowly from one side to the other.
4   To move around noisily in the bottom of a container, or to cause liquid to move around in this way by making rough movements.
5   To make someone extremely angry.
8   To speak or say something with unusual pauses or repeated sounds, either because of speech problems or because of fear and anxiety.
9   To shine in such a way that the light seems to shake slightly and quickly.
10 To go to another place to get something or someone and bring them back.
12 To repeat of sing a religious prayer or song to a simple tune.

Comprehension Quiz

1. Why did the seagulls start to fly faster?

A. They wanted to get away from the scary Cloud-men

B. They wanted to go to New York City

C. They wanted to have a race

D. They felt better after a cool shower

2. What did the travelers not see?

A. A snow machine

B. Frost factories

C. Drums for making thunder

D. Rain

3. What activities happened in the Cloud-Men's City? (two answers)

A. Wives fried snowballs for their husband's dinner

B. Children fought with each other

C. Children threw hailstones at the peach

D. Children went tobogganing down the clouds

Chapter 31

4. What was the last creature the travelers met that night?

A. A giant seagull leading the peach seagulls

B. A giant Cloud-Man jumping at the peach

C. A giant gray batlike creature which spread the night

D. A real giant bat

Comprehension Quiz

1. How do the travelers know where they are? (two answers)

A. It does not look like England

B. They are guessing

C. America is famous for skyscrapers

D. There is a sign that says "Welcome to New York City"

2. How are they going to get down?

A. Miss Spider and Silkworm will make ropes for everyone to climb down

B. The travelers will tell the seagulls to land the peach

C. The Centipede will cut some of the seagulls loose so the others will have to go down

D. They will sing so some of the seagulls will be sleepy and the peach will go down

3. What did everyone in New York City think the peach was?

A. A flying peach from Spain

B. A bomb from an enemy country

C. A balloon from the fair

D. A blimp from the football game

Chapter 32-33

4. Put the events in order. (-   -   -   )

A. Everyone took cover in the subway.

B. The President called his Admirals and Generals

C. Air-raid sirens went off

D. The Mayor of New York called the President

Comprehension Quiz

1. How many seagulls did the Centipede cut away?

A. One

B. Two

C. Three

D. Four

2. What happened when the airplane passed twenty feet over the traveler's heads?

A. It blew hot air on the peach and burned it up

B. It cut all of the seagulls loose

C. It bounced the peach and the travelers fell off

D. It radioed that the bomb was really just a peach

3. With no seagulls what was the peach like?

A. A jet airplane

B. A ticking bomb

C. An exciting roller coaster

D. A tumbling lump of lead

4. What did people not do when the "bomb" fell?

A. Say good-bye to each other

B. Get on their knees and pray

C. Stare in shock

D. Run faster for the subway

Chapter 34-36

5. On which building did the peach get stuck?

A. The Sears Tower

B. The Patronas Towers

C. The Empire State Building

D. The Statue of Liberty

Comprehension Quiz

1. What did the people not think?

A. It is a flying saucer

B. They are from Outer Space

C. They are giant bugs on a giant peach

D. They are from Mars

2. Where did the police and firefighters go?

A. Into a taller building to look down on the peach

B. Up to the observation roof below the needle

C. Into helicopters so they could look closely from the top

D. Into the subway so they could get away

3. What did the police not think the Centipede was?

A. A Gorgon

B. A Sea-serpent

C. A Cockatrice

D. A Manticore

4. What happened when the Old Green Grasshopper looked over the edge of the peach?

A. One person took a picture

B. The chief of police shot at the grasshopper

C. Six strong men jumped off of the building

D. Six strong men fainted

Chapter 37

5. What do the men think the spider eats for breakfast?

A. Candy

B. Giant peaches

C. Fully grown men

D. One elephant

6. Who is braver the Head of the Fire Department or the Chief of Police?

A. The Head of the Fire Department

B. The Chief of Police

C. They are both brave

D. Neither one is brave

7. Match the giant bug with the job that James suggests

A. Centipede	a. Digging sewers
B. Worm	b. Sewing and knitting
C. Grasshopper	c. Bring her 400 children
D. Glow-worm	d. Make a dress
E. Spider	e. Play a tune
F. Ladybug	f. Replace electricity
G. Silkworm	g. Going to the nursery

Comprehension Quiz

1. What did the steeplejacks do?

A. They ate the peach

B. They took pictures of the peach

C. They lowered the peach

D. They blew up the peach

2. What did the steeplejacks not use?

A. Pulleys

B. Cranes

C. Ropes

D. Ladders

3. What were the people throwing out of the windows? (two answers)

A. Desks

B. Computers

C. White paper

D. Ticker tape

4. Who ate the peach?

A. The giant bugs

B. James

C. The mayor and all of the important people in the limousines

D. A mile of children following the peach

Chapter 38

5. Why did James love seeing so many children?
(two answers)

A. Because they could help eat the peach
B. Because he had been so lonely with Aunt Spiker and Aunt Sponge
C. Because they were cheering for him
D. Because he could make so many new friends

Comprehension Quiz

1. What Jobs did the travelers get?

A. Centipede • • a. Played in an orchestra
B. Earthworm • • b. Married Head of the Fire Department
C. Silkworm and Miss Spider • • c. Lived in the giant peach stone
D. Glow-worm • • d. Made Vice-President of sales
E. Old Green Grasshopper • • e. Started a nylon rope factory
F. Ladybug • • f. Lit the Statue of Liberty's torch
G. James • • g. Advertised women's face cream on TV

2. Where did James live?

A. Inside the peach
B. With the ladybug
C. In Aunt Sponge's and Aunt Spiker's old house
D. In the giant peach stone (seed)

Chapter 39

3. Who does the book say wrote the story?

A. Roald Dahl

B. The Old Green Grasshopper

C. The old man who gave James the bag of magic

D. James Henry Trotter

Build your Vocabulary

Chapter 31

- **skim** [skim] *v.* 스쳐지나가다, 미끄러지듯 가다; *n.* 피막, 얇은 층
  To move quickly just above a surface without touching it.

- **glimpse** [glimps] *n.* 흘끗 보임, 일견
  If you get a glimpse of something, you see them very briefly and not very well.

- **sinister** [sínistər] *a.* 불길한, 재수 없는, 재앙이 되는
  Making you feel that something bad or evil might happen.

- **funnel** [fʌ́nl] *n.* 깔때기; (깔때기꼴의) 환기통, 채광 구멍; 굴뚝
  An object which has a wide round opening at the top, sloping sides, and a narrow tube at the bottom, used for pouring liquids or powders into containers with narrow necks.

- **billow** [bilóu] *vi.* 크게 굽이치다; 부풀다; *n.* 큰 물결
  (billowy *a.* 놀치는, 크게 굽이치는)
  When smoke or cloud billows, it moves slowly upwards or across the sky.

- **crouch** [kráutʃ] *v.* 몸을 구부리다, 쭈그리다, 웅크리다
  To bend your knees and lower yourself so that you are close to the ground and leaning forward slightly.

- **frisk** [frisk] *v.* (경쾌하게) 뛰어다니다[놀다]; (가볍게) 뒤흔들다
  To move around in a happy, energetic way.

- **toboggan** [təbágən] *n.* 터보건 (썰매); (물가·사람의 운명 등의) 급락
  An object used for sliding over snow and ice which consists of a low frame on which a person or people sit.

- **whoosh** [hwú(:)ʃ] *n.* (의성어) 휙[쉭]; *v.* 쉭 하고 움직이다
  Used to describe something that happens very fast, with no pauses or delay.

- **swoop** [swú:p] *v.* 내리 덮치다, 급강하하다
  To move suddenly down through the air.

- **flap** [flæp] *v.* 펄럭이게 하다, 휘날리다, 퍼덕이다; *n.* 펄럭임, 퍼덕거림; 혼란, 소동
  To wave something, especially wings when or as if flying.

- **utter** [ʌ́tər] ① *a.* 완전한, 전적인 ② *v.* (소리·말·탄식 등을) 입 밖에 내다, 발언하다
  If someone utters sounds or words, they say them.

- **melancholy** [méləŋkàli] *n.* 우울, 울적함; *a.* 우울한, 슬픈
  Sad.

Chapter 31-39

Chapter 32

- **cramp** [kræmp] *v.* 속박하다, 제한하다, 가두다; *n.* 꺾쇠, 죔쇠
  To limit someone, especially to prevent them from enjoying a full life.

- **beetle** [bíːtl] *n.* [곤충] 딱정벌레, 갑충
  An insect with a hard shell-like back.

- **soot** [suːt] *n.* 검댕, 매연; *v.* 검댕으로 더럽히다, 검댕투성이로 하다
  A black powder that is produced when coal, wood, etc. is burnt.

- **skyscraper** [skáiskèipər] *n.* 고층건물, 마천루
  A very tall modern building, usually in a city.

Chapter 33

- **pandemonium** [pæ̀ndəmóuniəm] *n.* 수라장, 대혼란(의 곳)
  A situation in which there is a lot of noise and confusion because people are excited, angry or frightened.

- **hover** [hʌ́vər] *v.* 하늘을 떠다니다, 비상하다
  To stay in one place in the air.

- **smithereens** [smìðəríːnz] *n.* (pl.) (구어) 산산조각, 작은 파편
  A lot of very small broken pieces.

- **wail** [wéil] *n.* 울부짖음, 비탄, 통곡; *v.* 울부짖다
  High-pitched mournful or complaining cry.

- **summon** [sʌ́mən] *v.* 소환하다, 호출하다
  To order someone to come to you.

Chapter 34

- **flock** [flɑk] *n.* (양·새·사람 등의) 떼, 무리, 다수; *v.* 모이다
  A group of sheep, goats or birds of the same type.

- **polish** [páliʃ] *v.* 닦다, 윤내다, 윤이 나다; *n.* 광택, 윤
  To rub something using a piece of cloth or brush to clean it and make it shine.

- **lump** [lʌmp] *n.* 덩어리, 덩이; *v.* 덩어리로 만들다
  A piece of a solid substance, usually with no particular shape.

Build your Vocabulary

Chapter 35

plummet [plʌ́mit] *vi.* 수직으로 떨어지다; 뛰어들다; *n.* 낚싯봉, 가늠추
To fall very quickly and suddenly.

stupor [stjúːpər] *n.* 무감각; 마비, 혼수; 인사불성; 망연자실
A state in which a person is almost unconscious and their thoughts are very unclear.

Chapter 36

taper off *phrasal v.* (구어) 차차 버리다

M 복습 **squelch** [skweltʃ] *n.* 찌부러뜨림; *v.* 짓눌러 찌부러뜨리다;
To stop something from growing, increasing or developing.

★ **pinnacle** [pínəkəl] *n.* 작은 뾰족탑; 꼭대기, 정점
A small pointed tower on top of a building, or the top part of a mountain.

Chapter 37

복습 **gape** [géip] *vi.* 입을 크게 벌리다; 멍청히 입을 벌리고 바라보다
To look in great surprise at someone or something, especially with an open mouth.

binocular [bənɑ́kjələr] *n.* (pl.) 쌍안경; *a.* 쌍안경의
A pair of tubes with glass at either end that you look through to see things far away.

CM 복습 **clutch** [klʌtʃ] *vt.* 꽉 잡다, 붙들다
To take or try to take hold of something tightly.

★ **hatchet** [hǽtʃit] *n.* (북아메리카 인디언들의) 전투용 도끼; 손도끼
A small axe.

Wampus [wámpəs] *n.* 프랑스 만화책에 등장하는 에일리언

Gorgon [gɔ́ːrgən] *n.* [그리스 신화] 고르곤 (머리카락은 뱀, 몸체는 멧돼지, 손은 청동으로 된 세 자매 중 한 명으로 특히 페르세우스에게 살해된 메두사를 의미한다.)

sea-serpent *n.* 바다뱀, 물뱀; 큰 바다뱀

prock 로알드 달이 자신의 작품 속에 창조한 생물. 번역서에는 '볼록볼록 귀신' 으로 번역되어 있다.

manticore 맨티코어 (인간의 얼굴에 붉은 피부, 사자 몸, 전갈 꼬리를 가진 상상 속 생물)

snozzwanger 로알드 달이 자신의 작품 속에 창조한 생물. 번역서에는 '킁킁왕 왕이' 라고 번역되어 있다.

whangdoodle 로알드 달이 자신의 작품 속에 창조한 생물. 번역서에는 '왕 일 알이' 라고 번역되어 있다.

commotion [kəmóuʃən] *n.* 동요, 소동
A lot of noise, confusion, and excitement.

cup [kʌp] *v.* 손을 잔 모양으로 만들다
To make your hands into the shape of a bowl.

oinck [ɔ́iŋk] (=oink) *n.* 돼지 울음소리; *vi.* 꿀꿀거리다
A written representation of the noise that a pig makes.

cockatrice [kákətris] *n.* 한 번 노려보기만 해도 사람이 죽는다는 전설상의 독사

stew [stjuː] *vt.* 약한 불로 끓이다; [요리] 스튜
To cook meat, fish, vegetables or fruit slowly and gently in a little liquid.

snakes and ladders *n.* (영) 뱀과 사다리 (주사위 놀이의 일종)
Children's game played on a board that has pictures of snakes and ladders.

scorpula 로알드 달의 작품 속 생물. 번역서에는 '살인 전갈(scorpion)'로 번역되어 있다.

vermicious knid 로알드 달의 작품 속 생물. 번역서에는 '맹독성 짜기벌레'로 번역되어 있다.

gruesome [grúːsəm] *a.* 소름 끼치는, 무시무시한; 힘든
Extremely unpleasant and shocking, and usually dealing with death or injury.

giddy [gidi] *a.* 현기증 나는, 아찔한
If you feel giddy, you feel unsteady and think that you are about to fall over.

overgrow [òuvərgróu] *vt.* 자라서 뒤덮다; 너무 커지다[퍼지다]
Covered with plants that are growing thickly and in an uncontrolled way.

chaperone [ʃǽpəròun] *n.* (사교계에 나가는 젊은 여성의) 여성 보호자, 샤프롱
An older person, especially a woman, who goes with and takes care of a younger woman who is not married when she is in public.

Build your Vocabulary

- **throne** [θróun] *n.* 왕위, 왕좌
  The special chair used by a ruler, especially a king or queen.

- **sewer** ① [sjú:ər] *n.* 하수구, 하수도 ② [sojú:r] *n.* 바느질하는 사람, 재봉사
  Someone whose job is to adjust, repair and make clothes.

- **boon** [bú:n] *n.* 은혜, 혜택, 이익
  Something that is very helpful and improves the quality of life.

- **fierce** [fíərs] *a.* 흉포한, 사나운, 맹렬한
  Physically violent and frightening.

- **smack** [smæk] *vt.* 찰싹 치다; *n.* 찰싹 하는 소리
  To hit something hard against something else so that it makes a short loud noise.

- **eccentricity** [èksentrísəti] *n.* (복장·행동 등의) 이상함, 엉뚱함; 기이한 버릇
  The state of being eccentric.

- **Miss Muffet** 대표적인 마더구스 중 하나인 Little Miss Muffet에 등장하는 인물

- **tuffet** *n.* 다리가 셋인 의자
  A piece of furniture used as a footstool or low seat.

- **nursery** [nə́:rsəri] *n.* 육아실, 탁아소, 보육원; 양성소, 훈련소
  A place where young children and babies are taken care of while their parents are at work.

- **entrance** [éntrəns] *vt.* 황홀하게 하다, 도취시키다
  If something or someone entrances you, they cause you to feel delight and wonder, often so that all your attention is taken up and you cannot think about anything else.

- **weave** [wí:v] *v.* (wove-woven) (직물을) 짜다, 엮다; 왔다갔다 움직이다
  To go or make a path by moving quickly and changing direction often.

Chapter 38

- **flabbergast** [flǽbərgæ̀st] *vt.* (구어) 소스라쳐 놀라게 하다, 당황하게 하다
  To shock someone, usually by telling them something they were not expecting.

- **steeplejack** [stí:pəldʒæ̀k] *n.* 뾰족탑[연돌] 수리공
  A person whose job is to climb high buildings in order to repair, paint, clean them, etc.

Chapter 31-39

- **procession** [prəséʃən] *n.* 행렬; 행진; 진행, 전진
  A series of people or things, one after the other.

- **hoist** [hɔ́ist] *vt.* 내걸다; 올리다, 감아올리다; 들어서 나르다
  To lift something heavy, sometimes using ropes or a machine.

- **skid** [skid] *v.* 미끄러지다; *n.* (무거운 물건을 굴릴 때 까는) 굴대, 미끄럼
  To slide along a surface so that you have no control.

- **swarm** [swɔ́ːrm] *vi.* 떼를 짓다; *n.* 떼, 무리
  When people swarm somewhere, they move there in a large group.

- **feast** [fiːst] *n.* 축제, 진수성찬 *v.* 축연을 베풀다, 진수성찬을 먹다
  A day on which a religious event or person is remembered and celebrated.

- **the Pied Piper of Hamelin** 피리 부는 사나이 (독일에서 출간된 그림 형제의 동화 중 하나)

- **descend** [disénd] *v.* 내려가다, 내리다
  To go or come down.

Chapter 39

- **torch** [tɔːrtʃ] *n.* 횃불, 호롱불
  A thick stick with material which burns tied to the top of it in order to give light.

- **haunt** [hɔːnt] *v.* 자주 가다, 빈번히 들르다; (유령이) 출몰하다; 늘 따라다니다
  To appear in a place repeatedly.

- **monument** [mánjəmənt] *n.* 기념비, 기념물
  A statue or building that is built to honour a special person or event.

- **gossip** [gásip] *n.* 잡담, 한담; 험담; (신문·잡지 등의) 가십
  Conversation or reports about other people's private lives which might be unkind, disapproving or not true.

Crossword Puzzle

Use the clues and the words in the box to complete the crossword puzzle.

utter	swoop	haunt	clutch	crouch	wail	hover	swarm
giddy	squelch	smack	gape	skim	glimpse		

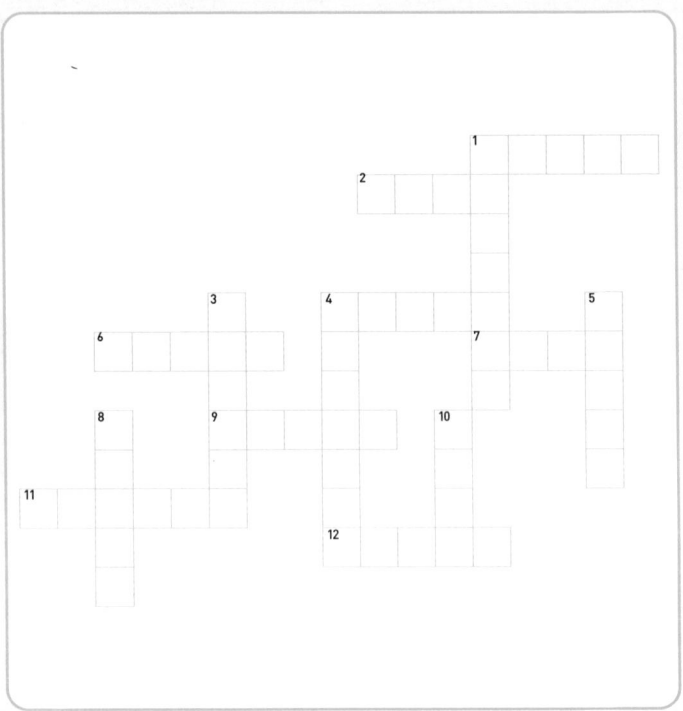

Across

1. If you feel _____, you feel unsteady and think that you are about to fall over.
2. High-pitched mournful or complaining cry.
4. To move suddenly down through the air.
6. When people _____ somewhere, they move there in a large group.
7. To move quickly just above a surface without touching it.
9. If someone _____s sounds or words, they say them.
11. To take or try to take hold of something tightly.
12. To stay in one place in the air.

Down

1. If you get a _____ of something, you see them very briefly and not very well.
3. To bend your knees and lower yourself so that you are close to the ground and leaning forward slightly.
4. Make a sucking sound like the one produced when you are walking on soft wet ground.
5. To hit something hard against something else so that it makes a short loud noise.
8. To appear in a place repeatedly.
10. To look in great surprise at someone or something, especially with an open mouth.

Answers

Comprehension Quiz Answers

Ch 1   1. C   2. B   3. A, D   4. D   5. B, C   6. C

ch 2   1. B   2. A   3. D   4. A, D

ch 3   1. B   2. A, B   3. C   4. D   5. B, C

ch 4   1. D   2. A, C   3. B   4. C

ch 5   1. C   2. D   3. A   4. D

ch 6   1. D   2. C   3. A   4. C   5. D   6. B

ch 7   1. D   2. A, B   3. A, D   4. B

ch 8   1. D   2. A, B   3. B   4. C   5. B

ch 9   1. C   2. C   3. C   4. B

ch 10   1. B, C   2. D   3. C   4. A

ch 11   1. D   2. C   3. A, C   4. B   5. B   6. D

ch 12   1. D   2. A   3. C   4. B   5. C

ch 13   1. B   2. C   3. D   4. B   5. C

ch 14   1. A, C   2. D   3. D   4. A, D

ch 15   1. A, D   2. C   3. B A D C

ch 16   1. C   2. D   3. B   4. D   5. A

ch 17   1. D   2. C   3. B   4. B   5. A

ch 18   1. B   2. C   3. A   4. D   5. D

ch 19   1. C   2. D C B A   3. B

ch 20   1. B   2. D   3. A, D   4. C   5. A

ch 21   No Questions

ch 22   1. A-c, B-a, C-d, D-e, E-b   2. B   3. D   4. B

ch 23   1. C   2. A, D   3. A, D   4. B   5. D

ch 24   1. C   2. B   3. D   4. A

ch 25   1. C, D   2. B   3. D   4. C   5. A

ch 26   1. B   2. C   3. D   4. C, D   5. A

ch 27   1. D   2. A, B   3. B   4. B A D C   5. A   6. B, C

ch 28   1. D   2. B   3. C   4. B C D A   5. D

ch 29   1. A   2. C, D   3. A, D

ch 30   1. C   2. D   3. C   4. D   5. C

ch 31   1. A   2. D   3. A, D   4. C

ch 32-33   1. A, C   2. C   3. B   4. C A D B

ch 34-36   1. D   2. B   3. D   4. D   5. C

ch 37   1. C   2. B   3. C   4. D   5. C   6. D   7. A-b B-a C-e D-f E-g F-c G-d

ch 38   1. C   2. B   3. C, D   4. D   5. B, D

ch 39   1. A-d B-g C-e D-f E-a F-b G-c   2. D   3. D

Crossword Puzzle Answers (Ch 1-5)

Across

1 filthy
2 wriggle
5 crouch
7 froth
9 ooze
10 peculiar
12 nasty
13 clutch
14 dainty

Down

1 fabulous
3 gulp
4 extraordinary
5 cruel
6 chop
7 flabby
8 hideous
11 waddle

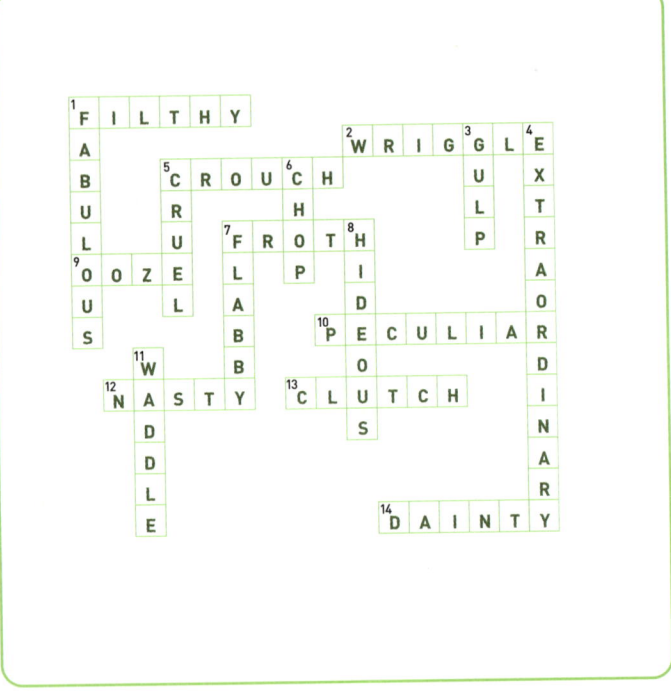

Crossword Puzzle Answers(Ch 6-10)

Across

1 soggy
3 groove
4 crawl
6 crafty
10 lick
11 glimpse
13 spellbound
14 gracious

Down

1 shiver
2 twinkle
5 hunk
7 tremendous
8 dazzle
9 swell
12 swarm
13 snap

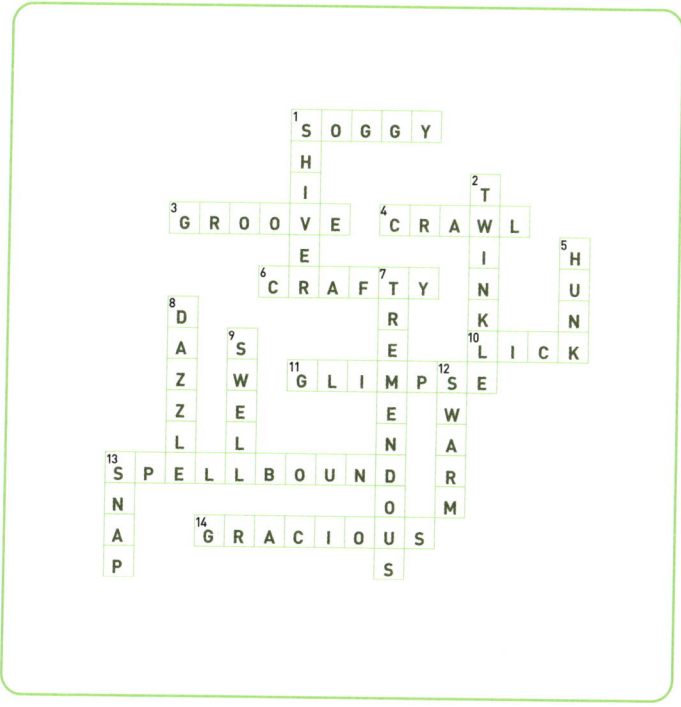

Crossword Puzzle Answers (Ch 11-15)

Across

4 wheeze
6 nibble
8 scarlet
9 wriggle
11 mumble
13 desolate
14 squat
15 tilt
16 horrid

Down

1 colossal
2 shiver
3 jostle
5 enormous
7 frantically
10 splendid
12 murmur

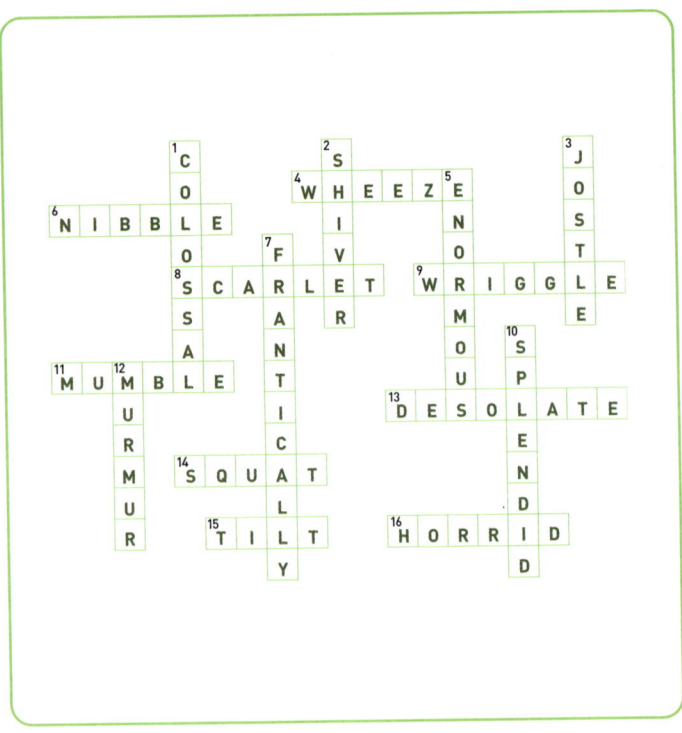

Crossword Puzzle Answers(Ch 16-20)

Across

1 absurd
5 filthy
6 glint
7 amidst
8 plunge
11 tangle
13 shriek
14 colossal

Down

2 rattle
3 cluster
4 disaster
5 fabulous
8 perish
9 smack
10 shrivel
12 gape

Crossword Puzzle Answers (Ch 21-25)

Across

1. scuttle
4. wriggle
6. fiddle
7. flabby
8. bulge
11. hollow
13. froth
14. gobble
15. crouch

Down

2. thread
3. spellbound
5. jiffy
7. frown
9. ghastly
10. hurl
12. thigh

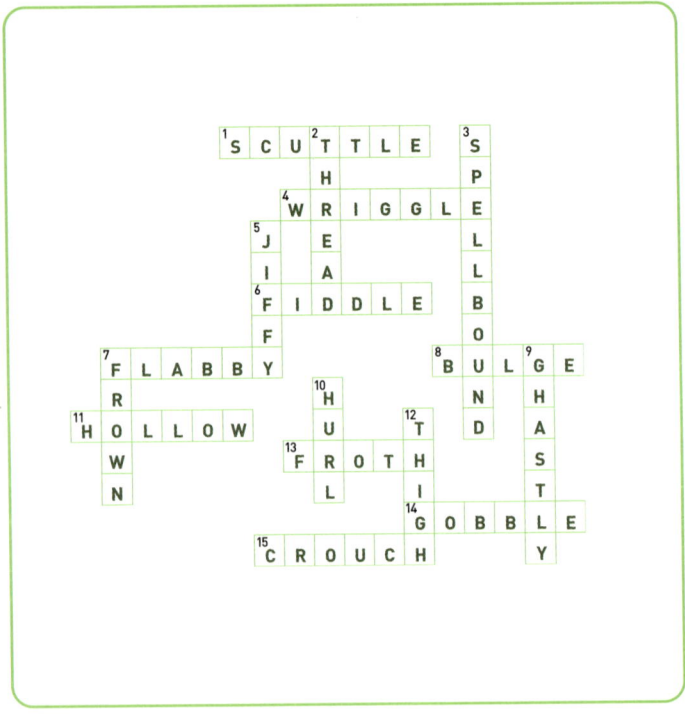

Crossword Puzzle Answers (Ch 26-30)

Across

6 whirl
7 squelch
11 frantic
13 huddle
14 tumble
15 swarm

Down

1 quiver
2 crouch
3 sway
4 slosh
5 infuriate
8 stammer
9 shimmer
10 fetch
12 chant

Crossword Puzzle Answers(Ch 31-39)

Across

1 giddy
2 wail
4 swoop
6 swarm
7 skim
9 utter
11 clutch
12 hover

Down

1 glimpse
3 crouch
4 squelch
5 smack
8 haunt
10 gape

James and the Giant Peach를 완독하셨군요! 축하합니다!

로알드 달의 다른 책도 꾸준히 읽어보세요.

James and the Giant Peach를 재밌게 읽으셨다면 Roald Dahl의 다른 대표작인 Charlie and the Chocolate Factory와 Matilda도 함께 읽어보세요. 같은 저자의 시리즈를 읽다보면 비슷한 문체와 어휘를 반복해서 만나게 되고, 이는 리딩 속도 향상과 어휘력 신장으로 자연스레 이어집니다. Charlie and the Chocolate Factory와 Matilda의 『원서 읽는 단어장』도 출간되어 있습니다. 인터넷 서점에서 '원서 읽는 단어장'을 검색해보세요.

무료 단어장을 받아보세요!

다른 원서를 읽을 때도 정리된 단어장이 있다면 정말 좋겠지요? www.readingtc.com/voca를 방문해보세요. 원서별로 어려운 어휘를 정리한 단어장 무료 PDF를 제공하고 있습니다.

모든 원서들의 단어장을 제공하고 있진 못하지만, 비교적 많이 읽히는 원서를 중심으로 꾸준히 업데이트 되고 있습니다. 새로운 원서를 읽기 전에 단어장이 준비되어 있지는 않은가 꼭 한번 확인해보세요!

함께 모여 원서 읽는 〈스피드 리딩 카페〉

어떤 원서를 읽을지 고민이신가요? 원서를 꾸준히 읽고 싶은데 잘 안 되시나요? 그럴 때는 함께 모여 원서를 읽는 〈스피드 리딩 카페 cafe.naver.com/readingtc〉를 방문해보세요. 수준별 추천 원서 목록, 함께 만든 원서별 단어장, 매월 진행되는 북클럽 등 원서 읽기에 도움이 되는 자료가 넘쳐납니다. 무엇보다 원서를 함께 읽을 동료들을 만날 수 있는 멋진 곳이랍니다! 이미 수천 명이 함께 모여 원서를 읽고 있지요. 원서 읽기에 관심이 있으시다면 이곳을 방문해서 함께 참여해보세요!

Text copyright © 2009 Longtail Books
James and the Giant Peach illustrations © 1995 Quentin Blake

이 책에 사용된 일러스트 사용 권한은 A P Watt Ltd를 통해 계약한 롱테일북스에 있습니다.
한국 내에서 보호받는 저작물이므로 무단 전재와 무단 복제를 금합니다.

원서 읽는 단어장
James and the Giant Peach

1판 1쇄 2009년 5월 4일
1판 10쇄 2024년 2월 19일

기획 이수영
책임편집 김수진
콘텐츠 제작 Michael Allen Misner · 롱테일 교육 연구소
마케팅 두잉글 사업 본부

펴낸이 이수영
펴낸곳 롱테일북스
출판등록 제2015-000191호
주소 04033 서울특별시 마포구 양화로 113, 3층(서교동, 순홍빌딩)
전자메일 help@ltinc.net

ISBN 978-89-5605-347-9 14740
　　　978-89-5605-319-6 (세트)